COUNT ME IN!

SEEKING OPPORTUNITIES TO SERVE

THE HOUSTON FIRE DEPARTMENT'S HOTTEST CHEFS SHARE THEIR SIZZLING SECRETS

COUNT ● ME IN!
THE HOUSTON FIRE DEPARTMENT'S HOTTEST CHEFS SHARE THEIR
SIZZLING SECRETS

Copyright © 2000
Houston Fire Department
Community Relations Division
601 Sawyer, Suite 301
Houston, TX 77007
713-865-4221

Editor: Lillian Harris

Library of Congress Number: 00-133365
ISBN: 0-9701523-0-2

Designed, Edited, and Manufactured by
Favorite Recipes® Press
An imprint of

FRP™

P.O. Box 305142
Nashville, Tennessee 37230
1-800-358-0560

Book Design: Pam Cole
Art Director: Steve Newman
Project Manager: Susan Larson

Manufactured in the United States of America
First Printing: 2000   5,000 copies

In Memory Of
Houston Firefighters

Lewis Mayo III and Kimberly Ann Smith

Contents

Contents

Special Thanks

Lester Tyra
FIRE CHIEF

Rick Flanagan
ASSISTANT CHIEF

Julissa Guerrero
PHOTOGRAPHER/
EDITORIAL ASSISTANT

Firefighter Bruce Mitchell
ARTIST

Captain David Almaguer
MEDILIFE

Firefighter Jeff Jacobs
Firefighter Glen Brannon
Captain Tommy Erickson
CONTRIBUTING WRITERS

About the Houston Fire Department

The Houston Fire Department, the third-largest fire department in the United States, follows the motto: Seeking Opportunities to Serve. This statement reflects what being a firefighter is all about—always ready to serve our community in so many ways. This motto is clearly imprinted on the sides of all of our fire apparatus that protect the lives and property of Houston citizens.

Our Mission Statement: The Houston Fire Department is a professional organization continually seeking opportunities to serve our community through fire prevention, emergency operations, patient care, and excellent customer care.

Proceeds from the sale of this book will be used to assist the elderly, disabled, and less fortunate in our city who cannot afford to protect their homes with smoke detectors. Our goal is to have every home in Houston protected with a working smoke detector and to continue to spread the vital fire safety message. In addition, if this book is successful, an additional donation will be made to the Last Alarm Club, a Houston organization designed to assist the families of deceased or severely injured Houston firefighters. Thank you for your donation to these two equally worthy causes.

Medilife of Houston, Inc., a non-profit organization dedicated to public awareness of emergency medical services care, EMS training, community CPR training and funding, and research, has been gracious enough to manage the funds for this book and has set up an account for the Houston Fire Department. Through the Board's approval, the funds will be used to purchase fire safety literature and smoke detectors. Thank you for helping to make this possible.

For more information on Medilife of Houston, Inc., contact David Almaguer at 713-865-4112.

From The Editor

Many years ago, I decided to create a cookbook for the Houston Fire Department. After eating at a few stations, I quickly learned that there are some very talented cooks who take pride in their creations. At least I have never heard any firefighters say they didn't like their meals at the fire station!

With a department as big as Houston, it seemed like it would be an easy task to compile some 100 recipes. I just never thought it would take five years to do it! With so many other projects pushing it aside, this cookbook quickly became a lower priority. Yet as time has moved along, firefighters have continued to ask, "When is that cookbook coming out?"

That cookbook is finally here and it is for you, the members of the Houston Fire Department, your family, and friends.

As you flip through this book, hopefully one of these meals will bring you back in time and to the table with your second family.

I hope you enjoy this book as much as I have enjoyed putting it together!

Lil Harris

About the Editor: Lillian M. Harris ("Lil") was with the Houston Fire Department from 1990 to 2000. As Public Information Officer in the Community Relations Division, she was editor of the departmental newsletter, *Houston Heat*, and managed the Public Information Section. She also coordinated many special events for the department.

About the Artist: Bruce Mitchell is a full-time firefighter with the Houston Fire Department. A twenty-year HFD veteran, Bruce has been drawing cartoons since he was in high school. As a teenager he accepted a part-time job at a botanical museum within walking distance from his high school, Spring Branch Senior High in Houston, Texas. That was where his talents were first discovered. When the directors noticed his talent for drawing, they asked him to help illustrate a botanical dictionary, "Indigenous Plants of Southwest Texas." Later, he became a machinist and soon became the company's newsletter artist when they discovered his cartoons of fellow employees. His illustrations have been included in two of the Houston Fire Department's commemorative books. His insight and talent for depicting firefighters at work is ingenious. The *Count Me In* Houston Fire Department cookbook is honored to include his work.

Special Thanks

Brian Harris
MY HUSBAND

Phil Harris, Ph.D.
WHOSE
ENCOURAGEMENT
NEVER CEASED

Houseton Fire Museum

**The Crews of Stations
7, 51, and 93
PHOTOGRAPHY SHOOTS**

All the firefighter chefs

who took the time to

share a favorite recipe

All the firefighters that

submitted their ideas

and input via email

Preface

The Houston Fire Department is proud of its history, a history that goes back over one hundred years. Established in 1838 as a volunteer fire brigade, HFD became a full-time paid department on Saturday, June 1, 1885.

In their first twenty-five years as full-time firefighters, the original forty-four men covered a nine-square-mile area and responded to emergencies on forty horse-drawn apparatus. The department consisted of seven fire stations.

By 1921, all forty horse-drawn steamers were replaced by motorized fire apparatus. The last horses in the department were retired to the Hermann Park Zoo in 1924.

On February 12, 1912, Houston firefighters responded to the largest fire in Houston's history—the Great Fifth Ward fire. Forty square blocks were destroyed—including a church, school, eight stores, thirteen industrial plants, twenty-nine two-story buildings, ninety single-story cottages, one-hundred and sixteen boxcars, nine oil tank cars, and at least forty thousand bales of cotton. Estimated damage exceeded five million dollars.

September 7, 1943, marked another tragedy for the city of Houston as fifty-five lives were claimed at the downtown Gulf Hotel fire. Thirty-six people were injured in the city's most deadly fire.

Four other historic fires remain lodged in firefighters' minds. The most recent is the McDonald's restaurant fire that claimed the lives of two firefighters, Lewis Mayo III and Kimberly Smith, on February 14, 2000. Five years earlier, the Houston Distribution Inc. Warehouse on Market Street was the largest single-building fire in Houston and burned the equivalent of three city blocks for two consecutive days, March 24 and 25, 1995. Remembered for its multiple fire deaths is the March 6, 1982, Westchase Hilton Fire on 9999 Westheimer. Twelve people lost their lives in this tragic fire. Finally, the city's largest fire since 1912 was the Woodway Square Apartment fire on 1501 Winrock. This fire destroyed three hundred and fifty apartments and damaged more than one hundred units. The day after this fire, Houston City Council passed an ordinance restricting the use of wood shingles in multiple dwellings.

Today the Houston Fire Department is the third-largest fire department in the United States. A department of 3,291 men and women serve a population of 1.8 million in a 617-square-mile area.

Introduction

Welcome to *Count Me In*, a Houston Fire Department cookbook filled with simple and unique recipes that go a long way! Anyone familiar with life at the fire station knows that those three words, "Count Me In," will guarantee you a place at the fire station table!

When you are invited to a Houston fire station to eat breakfast or supper (the two most important meals), you better let the cook know right away if you are "in or out." Usually this lets the cook know how much food to prepare. But firehouse cooks have their own deadlines, so it's really important to find them quickly and impress them with the phrase, "Count Me In!" Most fire stations crews will feed you for free if you are a guest, but it's always a good idea to offer, and if you want to be welcomed back, bring a gallon of Blue Bell ice cream. Firefighters, of course, are expected to pay their fair share, as determined by the cook.

While gathered around the table, the subject of conversation may make you lose your appetite or may leave you scratching your head in confusion. While we can make no promises against your loss of appetite, it is our goal not only to share some favorite recipes from the kitchens of 87 Houston fire stations but to share some history, trivia, and terms in this book that will help to keep you in the conversation and explain what makes the Houston Fire Department so unique. The fire service is a career like no other.

Children of all ages, and even adults, continue to be fascinated with the mystique of the fire service and those sparkling bright red engines racing to assist those who have called for help. We hope that through the anecdotes and recipes woven into the fibers of the book you will hear the laughter within the station walls and smell the aromas that define the camaraderie and the very existence of the Houston Fire Department.

44's Armadillo Eggs

2 QUARTS PICKLED JALAPEÑO
   CHILES
16 OUNCES CREAM CHEESE,
   SOFTENED
1 POUND PORK SAUSAGE

12 OUNCES COLBY JACK CHEESE,
   SHREDDED
2½ CUPS BAKING MIX
1 (6-OUNCE) PACKAGE PORK
   FLAVOR SHAKE'N BAKE

Cut the tops off the chiles and remove the pulp, reserving the tops, pulp and seeds and discarding the stems. Stuff each chile with some of the cream cheese.

Combine the sausage, cheese and baking mix in a bowl and mix well. Shape the dough into 1½-inch balls.

Roll one of the balls into a thin rectangle on a lightly floured surface. Wrap around a stuffed chile, sealing the edges. Coat with the Shake'n Bake. Place on a baking sheet sprayed with nonstick cooking spray. Repeat the process with the remaining ingredients.

Bake at 300 degrees for 30 minutes. Cool on a wire rack. You may freeze these appetizers.

You may make a hot sauce with the reserved chile tops, pulp and seeds. Combine with 1 chopped onion in a saucepan. Add 16 ounces of shredded carrots or enough to cover the jalapeño juice. Bring the mixture to a boil. Let stand until cool. Spoon into a blender and process until of the desired consistency.

YIELD: APPROXIMATELY 32

J. T. BOND
STATION 44

Fire Station Names

Fire stations are better known to Houston firefighters as the number of the station with an "s" attached to the end. For example, "I work at 44's (fire station)."

Bacon-Stuffed Mushrooms

2 TO 4 (16-OUNCE) PACKAGES
    MUSHROOMS
1 OR 2 (16-OUNCE) PACKAGES
    BACON SLICES
1 BUNCH GREEN ONIONS,
    FINELY CHOPPED

2 OR 3 MEDIUM JALAPEÑO
    CHILES, FINELY CHOPPED
48 OUNCES CREAM CHEESE,
    SOFTENED
SEASONED BREAD CRUMBS

Rinse the mushrooms and pat dry. Remove the stems and chop. Place in a large bowl. Set the mushroom caps aside.

Cook the bacon in a skillet until crisp. Place on paper towels to drain; crumble. Add to the mushroom stems. Add the green onions, chiles and cream cheese to the mushroom stems and mix well.

Spoon a small amount of the cream cheese mixture into each mushroom cap. Arrange the filled mushroom caps on a baking sheet. Sprinkle with the bread crumbs.

Bake at 350 degrees for 20 minutes. Cool on a wire rack for 10 minutes. Serve immediately. You may reheat in a microwave for 30 to 45 seconds per serving.

YIELD: VARIABLE

TONI CARTWRIGHT
COMMUNICATIONS

Houston Fire Department

The Houston Fire Department has 87 fire stations, 82 engines, 34 ladder trucks, 10 aircraft fire crash units, 62 ambulances, 3 hazardous materials response units, 1 foam pumper, 2 rescue trucks, 10 evacuation boats, and 5 rescue boats.

Flaming Hot Buffalo Wings

1 POUND CHICKEN DRUMETTES
1/4 TO 1/2 CUP HOT PEPPER SAUCE
1 TABLESPOON
   WORCESTERSHIRE SAUCE
1 TEASPOON PAPRIKA
1/8 TO 1/4 TEASPOON CAYENNE
   PEPPER

1 TEASPOON PAPRIKA
BLEU CHEESE OR RANCH
   SALAD DRESSING
CELERY STICKS

Combine the drumettes, hot pepper sauce, Worcestershire sauce, 1 teaspoon paprika and cayenne pepper in a sealable plastic bag. Seal the bag and shake until the chicken is well coated. Chill for 30 minutes or longer; drain.

Arrange the drumettes in a single layer in a shallow baking pan. Sprinkle with 1/2 teaspoon of the paprika. Bake at 425 degrees for 10 minutes. Turn drumettes over. Sprinkle with the remaining 1/2 teaspoon paprika. Bake for 10 minutes or until cooked through.

Pour the dressing into a bowl. Arrange the drumettes and celery sticks on a serving platter. Serve with the dressing.

YIELD: 4 TO 6 SERVINGS

MICHAEL S. PLUMMER
FIRE ALARM

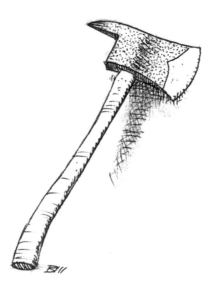

7-Alarm Jalapeño Cheese Squares

1 (6-OUNCE) CAN CHOPPED JALAPEÑO CHILES
16 OUNCES SHARP CHEDDAR CHEESE, SHREDDED
6 EGGS, BEATEN

Sprinkle the jalapeño chiles over the bottom of a greased 9×9-inch baking pan. Sprinkle the cheese over the chiles. Pour the eggs over the layers. Bake at 350 degrees for 30 minutes. Let stand until slightly cooled. Cut into squares.

YIELD: 8 TO 10 SERVINGS

GABINO "GABE" CORTEZ
ARSON

Arson Crime Lab

The Houston Fire Department Arson Crime Lab is recognized nationwide as one of the leading law enforcement labs in analyzing fire scene fingerprint evidence. A full-time polygraph examiner, who is also an investigator, examines latent prints and processes evidence. The Crime Lab receives daily submissions of evidence from arson cases and other outside agencies throughout Texas.

Station 103's Cheese Ball

8 OUNCES CREAM CHEESE, SOFTENED
3 OUNCES CREAM CHEESE WITH CHIVES, SOFTENED
4 OUNCES BLEU CHEESE, CRUMBLED
1/2 CUP (1 STICK) BUTTER, SOFTENED
2 TABLESPOONS FINELY CHOPPED CELERY
1 SMALL GREEN ONION, FINELY CHOPPED
2/3 CUP FINELY CHOPPED BLACK OLIVES
CRUSHED PRETZELS OR CHOPPED NUTS

Combine the cream cheese, bleu cheese, butter, celery, green onion and olives in a bowl and mix well. Shape into a ball. Roll in crushed pretzels in a shallow dish to coat. Chill, covered, until ready to serve.

YIELD: 12 TO 14 SERVINGS

KENNETH M. BOLES
STATION 103

Pineapple Cheese Ball

16 OUNCES CREAM CHEESE, SOFTENED
1 (8-OUNCE) CAN CRUSHED PINEAPPLE, DRAINED
1/4 CUP CHOPPED GREEN BELL PEPPER
1/2 CUP CHOPPED ONION
1 TEASPOON SEASONED SALT
1 CUP CRUSHED PECANS

Combine the cream cheese, pineapple, bell pepper, onion and seasoned salt in a bowl and mix well. Shape into a ball. Chill, covered, until firm. Roll in the pecans in a shallow dish to coat. Chill, covered, until ready to serve.

YIELD: 12 TO 14 SERVINGS

LIL HARRIS
PUBLIC INFORMATION

Artichoke Dip

2 (6-OUNCE) CANS CHOPPED
  ARTICHOKES
1 CUP MAYONNAISE
½ CUP GRATED PARMESAN
  CHEESE

8 OUNCES MOZZARELLA CHEESE,
  SHREDDED
½ CUP CHOPPED ONION
GARLIC SALT TO TASTE
BREAD CRUMBS

Combine the artichokes, mayonnaise, Parmesan cheese, mozzarella cheese, onion and garlic salt in a bowl and mix well. Spoon into a baking dish. Sprinkle with bread crumbs. Bake at 350 degrees until the bread crumbs are brown and the dip is heated through. Serve with crackers.

YIELD: 16 (2-TABLESPOON) SERVINGS

LINDA HONEYCUTT
RETIRED

Chili Con Queso Dip

1 POUND GROUND BEEF
GARLIC POWDER
1 (10-OUNCE) CAN TOMATOES
  WITH GREEN CHILES

1 POUND MILD VELVEETA
  MEXICAN CHEESE, CUBED

Brown the ground beef with a large amount of garlic powder in a skillet, stirring until crumbly; drain. Combine the cooked beef, tomatoes and cheese in a slow cooker. Cook on Low until the cheese is melted, stirring occasionally. Cook until heated through. Serve with tortilla chips.

YIELD: 42 (2-TABLESPOON) SERVINGS

DINA LIRA
ACCOUNTING

Seven-Layer Taco Dip

½ CUP MAYONNAISE

½ CUP SOUR CREAM

½ ENVELOPE TACO SEASONING
   MIX

1 (11-OUNCE) CAN BEAN DIP

1 (8-OUNCE) PACKAGE FROZEN
   AVOCADO DIP, THAWED

1½ CUPS SHREDDED CHEDDAR
   CHEESE

1 (4-OUNCE) CAN CHOPPED
   BLACK OLIVES

2 MEDIUM TOMATOES, CHOPPED,
   DRAINED

1 BUNCH GREEN ONIONS,
   CHOPPED

SHREDDED CHEDDAR CHEESE

Combine the mayonnaise, sour cream and taco seasoning in a bowl and mix well. Layer the bean dip, avocado dip, mayonnaise mixture, 1½ cups cheese, olives, tomatoes and green onions in a 9-inch pie plate. Sprinkle shredded cheese over the top. Chill, covered, for 2 hours or longer.

YIELD: 10 TO 12 SERVINGS

CHERYL MORRIS
EMERGENCY OPERATIONS

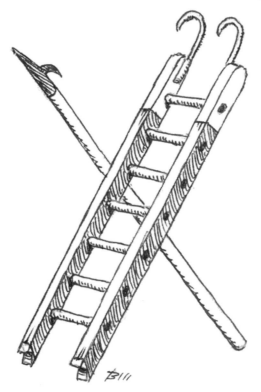

Green Tomatillo Sauce

15 OR 16 TOMATILLOS, PEELED
3 JALAPEÑO OR SERRANO CHILES
3 GARLIC CLOVES
½ ONION, CHOPPED

CILANTRO TO TASTE
2 AVOCADOS, CUT INTO PIECES
SOUR CREAM TO TASTE (OPTIONAL)
SALT TO TASTE

Place the tomatillos and chiles in a saucepan. Add enough water to cover. Cook until tomatillos are tender; do not boil. Drain the tomatillos and chiles. Remove the stems from the chiles. Process the tomatillos, chiles, garlic, onion, cilantro, avocados, sour cream and salt ⅓ at a time in a blender for 10 to 15 seconds or until smooth. Serve with chips.

YIELD: 12 (2-TABLESPOON) SERVINGS

KEN BOLES
STATION 103

Ready-to-Roll Picante Sauce

2 (15-OUNCE) CANS STEWED
  TOMATOES
¼ BUNCH CILANTRO
½ ONION, CHOPPED

½ TEASPOON MINCED GARLIC
½ TEASPOON SALT
1 TEASPOON SUGAR
1 TO 3 JALAPEÑO CHILES, SEEDED

Combine the tomatoes, cilantro, onion, garlic, salt, sugar and chiles in a blender container. Process until of the desired consistency. Serve with tortilla chips.

YIELD: 30 (2-TABLESPOON) SERVINGS

KEN BOLES
STATION 103

Fire Station 7 has traditionally been known among Houston firefighters as one of the "hottest" stations. For years, it has consistently remained one of the top-five busiest stations. Located just south of downtown, the station is nestled between Houston's scenic skyline downtown district and Houston's Medical Center. Its first alarm response area includes downtown, midtown, Montrose, Third Ward, Fourth Ward, and the Medical Center. In 1999, the historic Station 7 celebrated its 100th birthday.

Hot Sauce

1 GALLON WHOLE TOMATOES, CHOPPED	1 TABLESPOON PEPPER
2 SPRIGS OF CILANTRO, FINELY CHOPPED	1 TABLESPOON MINCED GARLIC, OR TO TASTE
6 OUNCES TOMATO PASTE	2 MEDIUM ONIONS, CHOPPED
¼ CUP SUGAR, OR TO TASTE	2 BELL PEPPERS, CHOPPED
1 TEASPOON SALT	4 TO 10 JALAPEÑO CHILES, SLICED

Cook the tomatoes in a large saucepan over low heat. Add the cilantro, tomato paste, sugar, salt, pepper and garlic and mix well. Steam the onions and bell peppers until tender. Add to the tomato mixture and mix well. Stir in the chiles. Cook for 30 to 45 minutes. Remove from the heat. Serve with chips.

Note: Use 4 to 6 jalapeño chiles for a mild sauce, 6 to 8 chiles for a hot sauce and 8 to 10 chiles for the hottest sauce.

YIELD: VARIABLE

MIKE A. GIRARDI
STATION 58

Hot Rod's Midtown Salsa

2 (28-OUNCE) CANS PEELED WHOLE TOMATOES	½ YELLOW ONION, FINELY CHOPPED
1 BUNCH CILANTRO, STEMS REMOVED	1 TEASPOON GROUND CUMIN
4 TO 7 FINELY CHOPPED SERRANO CHILES	1 TEASPOON GARLIC SALT
JUICE OF 1 LEMON	½ TEASPOON SALT
	½ TEASPOON PEPPER

Drain 1 can of tomatoes. Combine the drained tomatoes, remaining can of undrained tomatoes, cilantro, serrano chiles, lemon juice, onion, cumin, garlic salt, salt and pepper in a food processor container. Process until of the desired consistency. Season with additional spices and chiles if desired.

YIELD: 56 (2-TABLESPOON) SERVINGS

STATION 7

Rapid Response Salsa

2 (28-OUNCE) CANS CHOPPED
    TOMATOES
1 BUNCH CILANTRO
1 LARGE ONION, CHOPPED
2 TO 4 JALAPEÑO CHILES,
    CHOPPED

SALT AND PEPPER TO TASTE
GARLIC CLOVES TO TASTE
CUMIN TO TASTE
CHILI PEPPER TO TASTE

Combine the tomatoes, cilantro, onion, jalapeño chiles, salt, pepper, garlic, cumin and chili pepper in a blender container. Process until chunky. Pour into a saucepan. Cook over low heat for 15 to 20 minutes or until heated through, stirring occasionally.

YIELD: 6 TO 8 SERVINGS

CLYDE GORDON
STATION 26

Feel-the-Heat Salsa

¼ ONION, CHOPPED
¾ CUP CHOPPED FRESH
    CILANTRO
JUICE OF ½ LIME
1 (28-OUNCE) CAN PEELED
    WHOLE TOMATOES, DRAINED
1 JALAPEÑO CHILE

1 SERRANO CHILE
1 TEASPOON SALT
1½ TEASPOONS TONY
    CHACHERE'S ORIGINAL
    SEASONING
1 TABLESPOON PEPPER

Combine the onion, cilantro, lime juice, tomatoes, jalapeño chile, serrano chile, salt, Tony Chachere's Original Seasoning and pepper in a blender container. Process until of the desired consistency.

YIELD: 14 (2-TABLESPOON) SERVINGS

TREY SLEET
STATION 68

Fire Station 68

Fire Station 68 opened in 1973 in the heart of southwest Houston and consistently ranks in the top five as one of Houston's busiest stations. Annually, the Medic unit responds to more than 4500 medical calls. Station 68 houses an engine, ladder truck, medic unit, booster, and an evacuation boat.

Shrimp Dip

9 OUNCES CREAM CHEESE, SOFTENED	1/4 CUP FINELY CHOPPED GREEN BELL PEPPER
1 CUP SALAD DRESSING	1/2 (8-OUNCE) BOTTLE FRENCH SALAD DRESSING
1 POUND SHRIMP, COOKED, CUT INTO BITE-SIZE PIECES	2 OR 3 DROPS OF TABASCO SAUCE
1/2 CUP FINELY CHOPPED CELERY	JUICE OF 1 LEMON, OR 2 TABLESPOONS LEMON JUICE
1/4 CUP FINELY CHOPPED ONION	1 TABLESPOON VINEGAR
1 GARLIC CLOVE, FINELY CHOPPED, OR GARLIC SALT OR GARLIC POWDER TO TASTE	SALT TO TASTE
	PAPRIKA TO TASTE

Combine the cream cheese, salad dressing, shrimp, celery, onion, garlic, bell pepper, French salad dressing, Tabasco sauce, lemon juice and vinegar in a bowl and mix well. Season with salt and paprika. Chill, covered, for 8 to 12 hours for enhanced flavor.

NOTE: This recipe was our invitation to many a party: "Brian and Erma come to the party and bring the Shrimp Dip." I didn't think I would ever share this, but the time has come to do so.

YIELD: 45 (2-TABLESPOON) SERVINGS

ERMA MCLEROY
WIFE OF BRIAN MCLEROY

Caramel Apple Dip

8 OUNCES CREAM CHEESE, SOFTENED	1 TEASPOON VANILLA EXTRACT
1/2 CUP PACKED BROWN SUGAR	1/2 TEASPOON MAPLE OR CARAMEL FLAVORING

Combine the cream cheese, brown sugar, vanilla and maple flavoring in a blender container. Process until smooth. Serve with sliced Granny Smith apples.

YIELD: 6 SERVINGS

EDDIE AND LISA HAVLICE
STATION 18

Simple Firehouse Fare

8 TO 10 OUNCES CREAM CHEESE,   1 (8-OUNCE) CAN FRUIT
     SOFTENED   COCKTAIL

Whip the cream cheese in a mixing bowl until smooth. Add the fruit cocktail and mix well. Chill, covered, for 1 hour. Serve with crackers, fresh fruit or vegetables.

NOTE: This works well in the summer after a grilled meal. It is refreshing, light and better than ice cream.

YIELD: 1½ CUPS   LARRY BLACK
                                        STATION 33

Pecans Scandia

½ CUP (1 STICK) BUTTER   4 CUPS PECAN HALVES
2 EGG WHITES   SALT TO TASTE
1 CUP SUGAR

Place the butter in a 10×15-inch baking pan. Melt in a 325-degree oven.

Beat the egg whites in a mixing bowl until foamy. Fold in the sugar. Add the pecans and mix well. Spoon into the prepared pan. Stir and spread evenly over the pan.

Bake for 30 minutes, sprinkling once with salt and stirring every 10 minutes. Let stand until cool. Break into pieces. Store in an airtight container.

YIELD: 3 DOZEN PIECES   CHERYL MORRIS
                           OPERATIONS COMMAND

Cooking at the Fire Station

Firefighter Larry (Ma) Black has been cooking at the fire station for 27 years. What is he most famous for? The two briskets he cooked at downtown's Station 1 in two propane grills without any wood or lava rock. The challenge was to create a tasty outcome, despite his lack of resources. "I set the briskets on fire a few times," he remembers. But in the end, they were delicious.

The Big One or a Multiple
Alarm—A fire or emergency
that needs additional
firefighters and equipment
to control the scene.

"After the Big One" Strawberry Cooler

JUICE OF ½ LEMON
1 CUP UNSWEETENED STRAWBERRIES
1 TABLESPOON HONEY
¾ CUP ORANGE JUICE
1 TO 2 CUPS ICE CUBES
1 FRESH WHOLE STRAWBERRY

Combine the lemon juice, strawberries, honey, orange juice and ice cubes in a blender container. Process on high for 30 seconds or until smooth and creamy. Pour into a cocktail glass. Garnish with the whole strawberry.

YIELD: 1 SERVING

JIM "BIG DOG" HARLING
VAL JAHNKE TRAINING ACADEMY

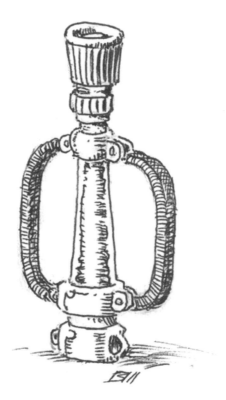

Eggnog

6 EGGS

1 CUP SUGAR

¼ TEASPOON NUTMEG

¼ TEASPOON CINNAMON

1 CUP HEAVY CREAM

2 CUPS MILK

¼ CUP RUM (OPTIONAL)

1 QUART VANILLA ICE CREAM

Beat the eggs in a mixing bowl until fluffy. Beat in the sugar, nutmeg and cinnamon. Stir in the heavy cream, milk and rum. Place the ice cream in a punch bowl. Pour the egg mixture over the ice cream.

NOTE: To avoid raw eggs that may carry salmonella, we suggest using an equivalent amount of pasteurized egg substitute.

YIELD: 12 TO 16 SERVINGS

CHERYL MORRIS
EMERGENCY OPERATIONS

APPETIZERS

City of Houston

The city of Houston is a 600-plus-square-mile area spread out over a 1000-square-mile triangular region in southeast Texas. It has a nighttime population of nearly two million people and a daytime population of over three million.

Kolaches

½ CUP WARM WATER	½ CUP EVAPORATED MILK
¼ CUP SUGAR	½ CUP VEGETABLE OIL
2 ENVELOPES DRY YEAST	1 TEASPOON SALT
1 CUP MILK	⅓ CUP SUGAR
4 EGG YOLKS	2½ CUPS (ABOUT) SIFTED FLOUR
2 CUPS (ABOUT) SIFTED FLOUR	

Combine the warm water and sugar in a bowl. Place the yeast in a small bowl. Pour the sugar water over the yeast; do not mix. Let stand for 15 minutes or until mixture is foamy.

Heat the milk in a saucepan until lukewarm. Beat in the egg yolks. Stir into the yeast mixture. Add 2 cups flour to make a soft dough and mix well. Let rise, covered, in a warm place for 30 minutes or until doubled in bulk.

Combine the evaporated milk, oil, salt, sugar and 2½ cups flour in a bowl and mix well. Add to the dough mixture and mix well. Knead on a floured surface until smooth and elastic. Place in a greased bowl, turning to coat the surface. Let rise until doubled in bulk.

Roll into a rectangle on a lightly floured surface. Cut into 1-inch slices. Arrange in a greased baking dish. Bake at 350 degrees until golden brown. Remove from the dish. Serve warm.

NOTE: This recipe has been around for many generations in the Beaty family. Boe doesn't make them often though, since it takes three to four hours to let the yeast rise. It's worth it though since firefighters devour them in minutes.

YIELD: 24 KOLACHES

BOE BEATY
STATION 71

Cinnamon Rolls

1 (16-OUNCE) LOAF FROZEN
    BREAD DOUGH, THAWED
1/4 CUP (1/2 STICK) BUTTER OR
    MARGARINE, MELTED
3/4 CUP PACKED DARK
    BROWN SUGAR

2 TABLESPOONS CINNAMON
1/2 CUP RAISINS
1/2 CUP PECANS, CHOPPED
1 CUP CONFECTIONERS' SUGAR
2 TABLESPOONS WATER

Roll the dough into an 8×14-inch rectangle on a lightly floured surface. Spread 2 tablespoons of the butter over the rectangle. Combine the brown sugar, cinnamon, raisins and pecans in a bowl and mix well. Sprinkle over the rectangle, leaving a 1/4-inch edge. Roll from the long side to enclose the filling, sealing the edge.

Cut the roll into 12 slices. Arrange in a lightly greased 9×9-inch baking pan. Spread the remaining 2 tablespoons butter over the tops. Chill, covered, for 6 hours. Let rise, covered, in a warm place until doubled in bulk.

Bake at 350 degrees for 20 to 25 minutes. Combine the confectioners' sugar and water in a bowl and mix until smooth. Drizzle over the warm rolls.

YIELD: 12 ROLLS

LARRY REISS
STATION 49

Aunt Ruby's Rolls

⅔ CUP SHORTENING

1 CUP HOT WATER

½ CUP SUGAR

1 CUP HOT WATER

1 TABLESPOON SALT

1 ENVELOPE DRY YEAST

1 CUP WARM WATER

5 TO 6 CUPS FLOUR

Place the shortening in a large bowl. Pour 1 cup hot water over the shortening. Let stand until the shortening is partially melted. Drain, reserving the liquid. Add the sugar to the shortening. Pour in 1 cup hot water. Let stand until the shortening is melted. Pour in the reserved liquid. Add the salt and mix well.

Dissolve the yeast in 1 cup warm water in a bowl. Add to the shortening mixture and mix well. Stir in enough flour to make a soft dough.

Place the dough in a greased bowl, turning to coat the surface. Let rise, covered, in a warm place until doubled in bulk. Punch the dough down. Let rise until doubled in bulk.

Shape into rolls. Arrange 1 inch apart on a baking sheet. Let rise until doubled in bulk. Bake at 350 degrees for 20 to 30 minutes or until golden brown.

YIELD: 30 TO 36 ROLLS

ROBERT HOGGARD
STATION 35

Darn Good Rolls

4 ENVELOPES DRY YEAST
½ CUP WARM WATER
2½ CUPS MILK
6 TABLESPOONS SUGAR
½ CUP SHORTENING
½ TEASPOON SALT
6 TO 6⅔ CUPS FLOUR

Dissolve the yeast in the warm water in a large bowl. Let stand until foamy. Bring the milk to a boil in a saucepan. Remove from the heat. Stir in the sugar, shortening and salt. Let stand until lukewarm.

Stir the milk mixture into the yeast mixture. Add 6 cups of the flour and mix well; dough will be sticky. Let stand, covered, for 15 minutes.

Shape the dough with greased hands into 1-inch balls for rolls or 2-inch balls for buns, adding ⅔ cup flour to dough if it is too sticky. Arrange the balls of dough on a greased baking sheet. Let rise, covered, for 15 minutes. Separate any rolls that are touching.

Bake at 450 degrees for 8 to 10 minutes or until golden brown. Serve hot with butter and honey.

YIELD: 3 DOZEN ROLLS

ROBERT BUCHMAN
STATION 101

Fire Station 101

Since opening Station 101, one of four stations serving Kingwood, I became the cook on the A-shift and this recipe was "introduced" to the guys at the station. The guys are always asking me to make those rolls for supper. One of the firefighters has a specific way of describing them, and because discretion is the better part of valor, those words cannot be printed.

—Robert Buchman

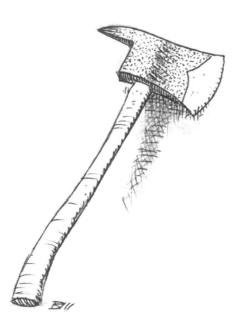

Station 6 sits just west of Houston's downtown on Washington Street. Consistently ranking as one of the top-ten busiest fire stations, this station serves Houston's "old" Sixth Ward, downtown, and everything south of the Heights community all the way to the Montrose area. It houses an engine, ladder truck, ambulance, and a chief's car. Because of its unique front and central location, visitors often tour this facility and photographers use it as a backdrop.

Corn Bread Casserole

2 (9-OUNCE) PACKAGES CORN MUFFIN MIX
2 (16-OUNCE) CANS CREAM-STYLE CORN
2 CUPS SOUR CREAM
2 EGGS, BEATEN
2 TABLESPOONS BUTTER, MELTED

Combine the muffin mix, corn, sour cream, eggs and butter in a large bowl and mix well. Spoon into a baking dish. Bake at 350 degrees for 40 to 45 minutes or until golden brown.

YIELD: 12 SERVINGS

KEVIN S. THERAULT
STATION 6

America's Best Morning Glory Muffins

2 CUPS FLOUR	¾ CUP FLAKED COCONUT
2 TEASPOONS BAKING SODA	½ CUP RAISINS
½ TEASPOON SALT	½ CUP PECANS
2 TEASPOONS CINNAMON	1 CUP VEGETABLE OIL
1¼ CUPS SUGAR	3 EGGS, LIGHTLY BEATEN
1½ CUPS SHREDDED CARROTS	½ TEASPOON VANILLA EXTRACT
2 LARGE APPLES, PEELED, SHREDDED	

Combine the flour, baking soda, salt and cinnamon in a large bowl and mix well. Stir in the sugar. Add the carrots, apples, coconut, raisins and pecans and mix well. Make a well in the center. Combine the oil, eggs and vanilla in a small bowl and mix thoroughly. Pour into the well. Stir into the dry ingredients just until moistened.

Spoon into 24 greased muffin cups, filling ¾ full. Bake at 375 degrees for 18 to 20 minutes or until golden brown.

YIELD: 2 DOZEN MUFFINS

ROBERT HOGGARD
STATION 35

Fire Station 35

Station 35 in southeast Houston serves the South Park community along MLK Boulevard. With an engine and an ambulance housed here, this station continues to remain one of the top-five busiest stations in Houston. That is probably why the ambulance is sometimes called "Cab Meals on Wheels"!

Banana Bread

½ CUP (1 STICK) BUTTER OR MARGARINE, SOFTENED

1 CUP SUGAR

2 EGGS

2 OR 3 BANANAS, MASHED

2 CUPS FLOUR

1 TEASPOON BAKING SODA

PINCH OF SALT

1 TEASPOON VANILLA EXTRACT

1 CUP PECANS

Cream the butter and sugar in a mixing bowl until light and fluffy. Add the eggs, bananas, flour, baking soda, salt and vanilla and mix well. Stir in the pecans.

Spoon into a greased loaf pan. Bake at 300 degrees for 1½ hours.

YIELD: 12 SERVINGS

RICHARD MANN
STATION 10

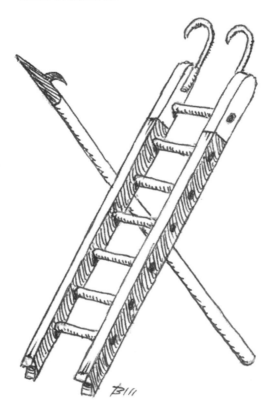

BREADS

Yeast Bread

3 ENVELOPES DRY YEAST
½ CUP LUKEWARM WATER
8 CUPS FLOUR
1 TO 1½ CUPS SUGAR

1 TABLESPOON SALT
1½ TO 2 CUPS LUKEWARM
WATER

Dissolve the yeast in ½ cup lukewarm water in a bowl. Let stand until foamy. Combine the flour, sugar and salt in a large bowl and mix well. Add the yeast mixture and enough of the 1½ to 2 cups lukewarm water to make a soft dough and mix well. Place in a greased bowl, turning to coat the surface. Let rise, covered, in a warm place for 1 hour or until doubled in bulk.

Knead on a floured surface until smooth and elastic. Divide the dough into 3 equal portions. Shape each portion into a loaf in a lightly greased loaf pan. Let rise until doubled in bulk.

Bake at 350 degrees for 15 to 20 minutes or until golden brown. Cool in the pans for 5 minutes. Remove from the pans. Slice and serve warm.

Pull-Apart Rolls: Shape the dough into 2-inch balls after kneading. Dust lightly with flour. Arrange in a greased baking pan. Let rise until doubled in bulk. Bake at 350 degrees until golden brown.

NOTE: Captain Billy Milliken always sits down at dinner with four to six pieces of bread and a whole stick of butter. He puts his dinner plate down with the bread surrounding the plate.

YIELD: 3 LOAVES   MIKE GIRARDI AND HOBERT HOGGARD
                                                  STATION 93

Fire Station 93's Cooks

These delicious rolls are a favorite at Fire Station 93. They are the only ones firefighters will eat. Firefighters Mike Girardi and Hobert Hoggard each joined the Houston Fire Department in 1977. Little did they know they would be cooking for 20 years. Although some firefighters can't eat a meal without Mike's homemade rolls and bread, his specialty is lasagna. "Chief Crowder likes it anyway," he says. With the approval of a Deputy Chief who has been eating at fire stations for 36 years, Mike considers that a compliment. Though he cooks just about everything, fellow firefighters say he can't make anything unless it has red sauce in it.

Sausage Loaf

1 (16-OUNCE) LOAF FROZEN
BREAD DOUGH, THAWED
1 POUND SAUSAGE

1 BELL PEPPER, CHOPPED
SHREDDED MONTEREY JACK
CHEESE

Place the dough in a greased bowl, turning to coat the surface. Let rise, covered, in a warm place for 1 hour or until doubled in bulk. Roll the dough into a rectangle on a lightly floured surface.

Brown the sausage with the bell pepper in a skillet, stirring until the sausage is crumbly; drain. Sprinkle over the dough. Sprinkle the cheese over the sausage mixture. Roll from the long side to enclose the filling, sealing the edge and ends.

Place seam side down on a baking sheet. Bake at 350 degrees for 45 minutes.

NOTE: As the #2 cook, firefighter Larry Vackar says he cooks when the #1 cook steps down. Cooking for more than 20 years at the fire station, he says one of his biggest requests is the Sausage Loaf. Chief Jerry Walker and Captain Red Blevins love it. (So, count on the chief checking by when the sausage loaf is in the oven!)

YIELD: 4 TO 6 SERVINGS

LARRY VACKAR
STATION 62

Stuffed Bread (Calzones)

4 POUNDS ITALIAN SAUSAGE
2 BELL PEPPERS, SLICED
1 MEDIUM ONION, SLICED
1 RECIPE YEAST BREAD DOUGH
    (PAGE 33)
2 POUNDS MOZZARELLA CHEESE,
    SHREDDED

2 (15-OUNCE) CANS HERB AND
    GARLIC TOMATO SAUCE
SALT AND PEPPER TO TASTE
MINCED GARLIC TO TASTE

Combine the sausage with enough water to cover in a saucepan. Bring to a boil. Boil until cooked through; drain. Cut into small pieces. Steam the bell peppers and onion until tender.

Roll the Yeast Bread dough into three ½-inch-thick 12-inch circles on a lightly floured surface. Sprinkle the sausage, bell peppers, onion and cheese over the circles. Pour the tomato sauce over the filling. Sprinkle with salt, pepper and garlic. Fold each circle in half to enclose the filling, sealing the edge. Place on a baking sheet.

Bake at 350 degrees for 30 minutes. Serve with additional tomato sauce.

YIELD: 3 CALZONES

MIKE A. GIRARDI
STATION 93

Lewis Mayo's Taquitos

2 POUNDS GROUND BEEF	BUTTER
½ RED BELL PEPPER, CHOPPED	12 EGGS, BEATEN
½ BELL PEPPER, CHOPPED	8 WARM FLOUR TORTILLAS
½ ONION, CHOPPED, OR	4 TO 6 CUPS SHREDDED
TO TASTE	CHEDDAR CHEESE

Brown the ground beef in a skillet, stirring until crumbly; drain.

Sauté the bell peppers and onion in a small amount of butter in a skillet. Stir in the eggs. Cook to the desired consistency, stirring constantly. Add the cooked beef and mix well.

Spoon the egg mixture down the center of each tortilla. Sprinkle with the cheese. Roll to enclose the filling.

YIELD: 8 SERVINGS   STATION 76

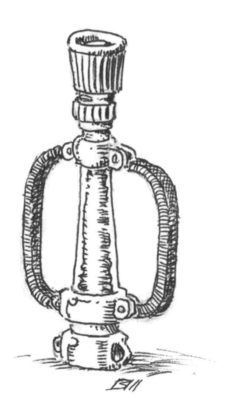

BREAKFAST

Firefighters' Breakfast

¼ CUP CHOPPED ONION

¼ CUP (½ STICK) BUTTER OR
    MARGARINE

2 MEDIUM POTATOES, PEELED,
    FINELY CHOPPED

1 TEASPOON WATER

¼ TEASPOON SALT

6 EGGS

2 TABLESPOONS MILK

¼ TEASPOON SALT

DASH OF PEPPER

1 CUP DICED COOKED HAM

Cook the onion in the butter in a skillet until tender. Add the potatoes, water and ¼ teaspoon salt. Cook for 10 minutes, stirring occasionally.

Beat the eggs, milk, ¼ teaspoon salt and pepper in a bowl. Stir in the ham. Pour over the potato mixture.

Cook over medium heat until the mixture begins to set; do not stir. Lift the cooked egg mixture, allowing the uncooked portion to flow under the cooked portion. Cook for 4 minutes or until completely set. Serve immediately.

YIELD: 4 SERVINGS

HARVEY BIRDWELL
STATION 62

When eating breakfast at a fire station, you can usually count on something very greasy; probably a 10 percent coronary blockage will develop just by smelling breakfast cooking! Sometime between 8:30 and 10 a.m., the designated firefighter/cook notifies the "watchman," who hurriedly announces over the PA system, "Breakfast is ready!"

In between calls, firefighters grab a plate, dispensing hefty portions and hoping the alarm is silent for just a few minutes. Inevitably, the alarm does often sound and you wind up shoveling as much food in as possible. This can often result in heartburn and a cold plate when you get back.

BREAKFAST

Roll Call Tacos

2 POUNDS SAUSAGE
1 MEDIUM ONION, CHOPPED
1 BELL PEPPER, CHOPPED
½ CUP (1 STICK) MARGARINE OR
   BUTTER
1 (32-OUNCE) PACKAGE FROZEN
   HASH BROWN POTATOES,
   THAWED

LEMON PEPPER
12 EGGS
1 (10-COUNT) PACKAGE FLOUR
   TORTILLAS

Brown the sausage in a skillet, stirring until crumbly; drain. Sauté the onion and bell pepper in the margarine in a skillet until tender. Sprinkle the potatoes with the lemon pepper.

Beat the eggs in a bowl. Stir in the sausage, onion mixture and potatoes. Pour into a nonstick skillet. Cook until the eggs are set, stirring frequently.

Spoon the egg mixture down the center of each tortilla. Fold to enclose the filling. Serve immediately.

YIELD: 10 SERVINGS

RICK BERLANGA
STATION 49

Camaraderie at the Fire Station

Meals are one of the best times of the day. It is more than just a time to eat. It is without a doubt the best time to develop and nourish the camaraderie we must have to exist in our environment. It's also the time for comic relief, our avenue of venting frustrations and obstacles we don't know how to face individually.

Firehouse Eggs

1 POUND SAUSAGE

8 SLICES BREAD, CUBED

16 OUNCES CHEDDAR CHEESE,
  SHREDDED

6 EGGS, BEATEN

3 CUPS MILK

¼ TEASPOON SALT

¼ TEASPOON CAYENNE PEPPER

¾ TEASPOON DRY HOT MUSTARD
  (OPTIONAL)

1 TABLESPOON TABASCO SAUCE

Brown the sausage in a skillet, stirring until crumbly; drain. Combine the sausage, bread, cheese, eggs, milk, salt, cayenne pepper, mustard and Tabasco sauce in a bowl and mix well.

Pour the egg mixture into a buttered 9×13-inch baking pan. Bake at 350 degrees for 1 hour. You may adjust the salt, cayenne pepper, mustard and Tabasco sauce to your taste.

NOTE: Very early on, I learned that food was a priority at the fire station. I used to be the official cook at Station 19.

YIELD: 11 SERVINGS

ROGER WESTHOFF
STATION 68

Scrambled Egg Omelet

24 EGGS

½ CUP MILK

1 RED BELL PEPPER, CHOPPED

8 OUNCES MEXICAN-STYLE VELVEETA CHEESE, DICED

Beat the eggs in a bowl. Add the milk and bell pepper and mix well. Cook the egg mixture in a large skillet until set, stirring frequently. Remove from the heat. Stir in the cheese. Let stand, covered, until the cheese melts.

You may substitute two drained 10-ounce cans tomatoes with green chiles for the red bell pepper.

YIELD: 10 TO 12 SERVINGS

LARRY BLACK
STATION 33

Daddy Rich's Quiche

1 UNBAKED (9-INCH) PIE SHELL
8 OUNCES SAUSAGE
18 SLICES BACON, CHOPPED
5 EGGS
2 CUPS HEAVY CREAM
1/8 TEASPOON SALT
3/4 TEASPOON PEPPER
8 OUNCES CHOPPED
    PRESSED HAM

1/2 CUP SHREDDED MOZZARELLA
    CHEESE
1/2 CUP SHREDDED SHARP
    CHEDDAR CHEESE
1/2 CUP CHOPPED ONION
1/2 CUP CHOPPED GREEN
    BELL PEPPER

Bake the pie shell at 425 degrees for 7 minutes or until golden brown.

Brown the sausage with the bacon in a skillet, stirring until the sausage is crumbly and cooking until the bacon is crisp; drain. Beat the eggs, cream, salt and pepper in a bowl.

Layer the sausage mixture, ham, mozzarella cheese, Cheddar cheese, onion and bell pepper in the pie crust. Pour the egg mixture over the layers.

Bake at 425 degrees for 15 minutes. Reduce the oven temperature to 350 degrees. Bake for 30 to 45 minutes or until a knife inserted in the center comes out clean. Let stand for 5 minutes. Cut into wedges to serve.

NOTE: This is an excellent dish and a fire station favorite.

YIELD: 6 SERVINGS

RAYMOND D. RICHARDSON
FIRE ALARM

Quiche Lorraine

12 SLICES BACON, CRISP-COOKED, CRUMBLED

1 CUP SHREDDED SWISS OR CHEDDAR CHEESE

1/3 CUP CHOPPED ONION

6 OUNCES SPINACH, CHOPPED

1 UNBAKED (9-INCH) PIE SHELL

4 EGGS, BEATEN

2 CUPS LIGHT CREAM

1/8 TEASPOON RED PEPPER

3/4 TEASPOON SALT

Layer the bacon, cheese, onion and spinach in the pie shell. Beat the eggs, cream, red pepper and salt in a bowl. Pour over the layers.

Bake at 425 degrees for 15 minutes. Reduce the oven temperature to 300 degrees. Bake for 30 minutes or until a knife inserted in the center comes out clean. Let stand for 10 minutes.

YIELD: 6 SERVINGS

ROBERT HOGGARD
STATION 35

Station 33's Manhole Covers

8 CUPS CAKE FLOUR

1 CUP SUGAR

½ CUP BAKING POWDER

1 TEASPOON BAKING SODA

1 TEASPOON SALT

8 CUPS BUTTERMILK

8 EGGS

Sift the flour, sugar, baking powder, baking soda and salt in a large bowl. Add the buttermilk and eggs. Whisk just until moist. Let stand for 5 minutes.

Pour ¼ cup at a time onto a 375- to 400-degree lightly greased griddle. Cook until brown on both sides, turning once.

You may reduce the recipe, decreasing the quantity of each ingredient by the same percentage.

YIELD: 6 DOZEN (4-INCH) PANCAKES

LARRY BLACK
STATION 33

Cinnamon Banana Waffles

2 CUPS BAKING MIX

1½ CUPS MILK

1 EGG

1 BANANA, MASHED

¼ TEASPOON CINNAMON

1 TEASPOON VANILLA EXTRACT

Beat the baking mix, milk, egg, banana, cinnamon and vanilla in a mixing bowl with a hand-held mixer until smooth. Cook in a waffle iron sprayed with nonstick cooking spray using the manufacturer's instructions.

YIELD: 6 WAFFLES

STATION 40—D SHIFT

Blowin' and Goin'—A fire where storm-like conditions brought on by the thermal columns are established. The fire actually churns, much like a tornado. Flames begin to dance within these thermal columns. There is not usually much smoke as it is a free-burning condition.

"Blowin' and Goin'" Chili Bean Soup

2 POUNDS GROUND SIRLOIN

1 LARGE ONION, CHOPPED

1 (3-OUNCE) CAN GREEN CHILES

2 (15-OUNCE) CANS PINTO BEANS

2 (15-OUNCE) CANS HOMINY

1 (15-OUNCE) CAN GREAT NORTHERN BEANS

3 (15-OUNCE) CANS TOMATOES

2 CUPS WATER

1 ENVELOPE TACO SEASONING MIX

1 ENVELOPE RANCH DRESSING MIX

Brown the ground sirloin in a 4-quart kettle, stirring until crumbly; drain. Add the onion, green chiles, pinto beans, hominy, Great Northern beans, tomatoes, water, taco seasoning mix and ranch dressing mix and mix well. Cook until heated through, stirring frequently.

You may substitute 3 ounces sliced jalapeño chiles or 3 ounces mild picante sauce for the green chiles to make the soup hotter.

Serve with flour tortillas.

YIELD: 10 TO 12 SERVINGS

LARRY MCCLURE
STATION 31

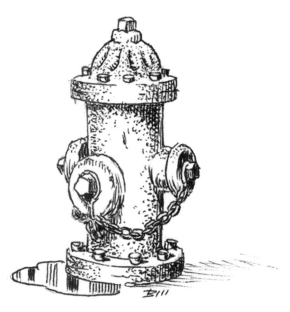

Texas Ranger Chili

3 POUNDS COARSELY GROUND LEAN BEEF	1 TABLESPOON SALT
3 CUPS (ABOUT) WATER	1 TABLESPOON BLACK PEPPER
2 LARGE ONIONS, FINELY CHOPPED	3 TABLESPOONS CHILI POWDER
3 GARLIC CLOVES, CHOPPED	2 TEASPOONS CAYENNE PEPPER
2 TABLESPOONS CUMIN	2 TABLESPOONS OLIVE OIL
1 TABLESPOON GROUND OREGANO	2 TABLESPOONS PAPRIKA
	1 (6-OUNCE) CAN TOMATO PASTE
	1 (12-OUNCE) CAN BEER
	MASA HARINA (OPTIONAL)

Brown the ground beef in a large cast-iron pot, stirring until crumbly; drain. Add enough water to just cover the beef.

Add the onions, garlic, cumin, oregano, salt, black pepper, chili powder, cayenne pepper, olive oil, paprika, tomato paste and beer and mix well.

Bring to a simmer. Cook for 2 hours, adding additional water a small amount at a time if chili is too thick. Stir in masa harina if chili is too thin and cook for an additional 15 minutes, stirring frequently.

NOTE: For the first time, Chief Jerry Walker divulges his secret that has earned him first-place ribbons at the San Antonio Fire Department's Chili Cookoff and at the Liberty County Chili Cookoff.

YIELD: 15 TO 18 SERVINGS

JERRY WALKER
STATION 6

Chili

Texas, The Lone Star State, is known for its award-winning chili cookoffs and contests. FYI: The official state dish is chili!

Low-Fat Turkey Breast Chili

1 (16-OUNCE) PACKAGE GROUND
    TURKEY BREAST
1 (10-OUNCE) CAN TOMATOES
    WITH GREEN CHILES
1 BELL PEPPER, CHOPPED
1 ONION, CHOPPED
2 (8-OUNCE) CANS TOMATO
    SAUCE
1 (6-OUNCE) CAN TOMATO PASTE

1 (16-OUNCE) CAN DARK RED
    KIDNEY BEANS (OPTIONAL)
BAY LEAVES TO TASTE
CHILI POWDER TO TASTE
CUMIN TO TASTE
GARLIC TO TASTE
SALT AND PEPPER TO TASTE
CLOVES TO TASTE (OPTIONAL)
BROWN SUGAR TO TASTE

Brown the ground turkey with the tomatoes, bell pepper and onion in a Dutch oven sprayed with nonstick cooking spray, stirring until the turkey is crumbly. Add the tomato sauce, tomato paste, kidney beans, bay leaves, chili powder, cumin, garlic, salt, pepper, cloves and brown sugar and mix well. Bring to a simmer.

Simmer the chili for 45 to 60 minutes. Remove the bay leaves. Serve with fat-free cheese and chopped green onions.

YIELD: 6 TO 8 SERVINGS

DEBBIE DAVIDS
FIRE CHIEF'S OFFICE

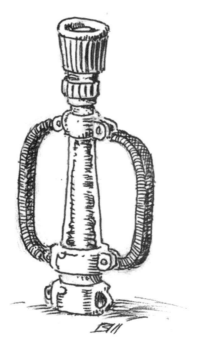

Healthy Firehouse Chili Soup

1½ POUNDS GROUND TURKEY
1 MEDIUM WHITE ONION, CHOPPED
3 (10-OUNCE) CANS MINESTRONE SOUP
2 (15-OUNCE) CANS STEWED TOMATOES
1 (10-OUNCE) CAN TOMATOES WITH GREEN CHILES
1 (15-OUNCE) CAN PINTO OR CHILI BEANS
3 SOUP CANS WATER

Brown the turkey with the onion in a large stock pot, stirring until crumbly. Add the soup, tomatoes, beans and water and mix well. Bring to a simmer. Cook for 10 minutes.

You may use tomatoes with oregano or Italian seasonings for a spicier chili. You may add cooked pasta, such as bowtie or shell, to increase the yield.

NOTE: When I made this at the station, I was expecting to have a lot left over. Boy, was I wrong! This will feed 16 people or 6 firefighters.

YIELD: 16 SERVINGS

LISA HAVLICE
STATION 18

Fire Station 18

Fire Station 18 is a bright spot on the near east side of Houston. When it comes to "curb appeal," this station wins! Citizens compliment the crews for the superb landscaping framing the fire station. Equipped with an engine, ladder truck, and Medic unit, this station responds to the Harrisburg and Lockwood communities and the University of Houston. Good meals are equally important at Station 18. Firefighters purchased a secondhand double electric oven and installed it themselves. Whatever it takes to cook a good meal!

Fast Attack Stew

16 OUNCES CARROTS, CHOPPED	1 LARGE ONION, CHOPPED
2 POUNDS POTATOES, CHOPPED	1 ENVELOPE BROWN GRAVY MIX
2 POUNDS BEEF, THINLY SLICED	2 TABLESPOONS KITCHEN
7 BEEF BOUILLON CUBES	BOUQUET
4 RIBS CELERY, CHOPPED	SALT AND PEPPER TO TASTE

Combine the carrots and potatoes in a large pot with enough water to cover. Bring to a boil. Boil until partially cooked; drain.

Combine the beef, bouillon cubes, celery and onion in a large pot. Add enough water to cover. Cook until the beef is tender.

Dissolve the gravy mix in a small amount of water in a bowl. Stir into the beef mixture. Stir in the Kitchen Bouquet. Cook for 5 minutes. Add the carrots and potatoes. Cook until the carrots and potatoes are tender and stew is heated through. Season with salt and pepper.

NOTE: Firefighter Gary Pick has been cooking at fire stations for 20 years. His biggest mistake was the day he asked the crew what they wanted to eat. He quickly learned that he had to be the one to make all the meal decisions. This dish is one of his most requested meals.

YIELD: 4 TO 6 SERVINGS

GARY PICK
STATION 7

Mexican Stew

5 POUNDS BEEF ROAST, CUBED

2 (16-OUNCE) CANS TOMATOES, CHOPPED

4 TO 6 GARLIC CLOVES, MINCED

6 TO 8 BEEF BOUILLON CUBES

1 ONION, CHOPPED

1 BELL PEPPER, CHOPPED

DASH OF CAYENNE PEPPER

PAPRIKA TO TASTE

CHILI POWDER TO TASTE

CUMIN TO TASTE

SALT AND BLACK PEPPER TO TASTE

4 YELLOW SQUASH, THINLY SLICED

4 ZUCCHINI, THINLY SLICED

4 EARS OF CORN ON THE COB, BROKEN INTO HALVES

6 POTATOES, CUBED

3 TABLESPOONS CHOPPED CILANTRO

Combine the beef, tomatoes, garlic, bouillon cubes, onion, bell pepper, cayenne pepper, paprika, chili powder, cumin, salt and black pepper in a large pot. Bring to a simmer. Cook until the beef is tender.

Add the squash, zucchini, corn, potatoes and cilantro and mix well. Cook until the potatoes and corn are tender. Remove from the heat. Let stand for 2 hours or longer to enhance the flavor.

Reheat the stew. Serve with corn tortillas and margarine.

YIELD: 15 TO 20 SERVINGS

JAMES LEDBETTER
STATION 7

Ravioli Soup

4 POUNDS GROUND SIRLOIN
1 CUP BREAD CRUMBS
1 CUP GRATED PARMESAN
    CHEESE
1 TABLESPOON ONION SALT
8 TEASPOONS MINCED GARLIC
¼ CUP OLIVE OIL
6 CUPS FINELY CHOPPED
    ONIONS
4 (28-OUNCE) CANS ITALIAN-
    STYLE CRUSHED TOMATOES

4 (6-OUNCE) CANS TOMATO
    PASTE
4 (15-OUNCE) CANS BEEF BROTH
2 TEASPOONS SUGAR
2 TEASPOONS BASIL
1 TEASPOON THYME
1 TEASPOON OREGANO
1 CUP CHOPPED FRESH PARSLEY
4 (12-OUNCE) PACKAGES FRESH
    CHEESE RAVIOLI
SALT TO TASTE

Brown the ground sirloin in a large pot, stirring until crumbly; drain. Add the bread crumbs, Parmesan cheese, onion salt, garlic, olive oil, onions, tomatoes, tomato paste, broth, sugar, basil, thyme, oregano and parsley and mix well. Bring to a boil. Reduce the heat. Simmer for 30 minutes or longer, stirring occasionally.

Cook the ravioli using the package directions; drain. Add to the soup and mix well. Season with salt. You may add additional broth for a thinner consistency.

YIELD: 12 SERVINGS

LARRY MCCLURE
STATION 31

Texas Taco Soup

3 POUNDS GROUND BEEF

2 OR 3 ENVELOPES TACO
    SEASONING MIX

2 ENVELOPES RANCH DRESSING
    MIX

2 (16-OUNCE) CANS WHOLE
    KERNEL CORN

2 (16-OUNCE) CANS WHOLE OR
    DICED TOMATOES

3 OR 4 (15-OUNCE) CANS PINTO
    BEANS

1 ONION, COARSELY CHOPPED

3 RIBS CELERY, CHOPPED

1 TO 2 CUPS PICANTE SAUCE

CHILI POWDER TO TASTE

GARLIC POWDER TO TASTE

SALT AND PEPPER TO TASTE

CUMIN TO TASTE

1 BUNCH CILANTRO, CHOPPED

SHREDDED CHEDDAR CHEESE
    TO TASTE

TORTILLA CHIPS

Brown the ground beef in a stockpot, stirring until crumbly; drain. Add the taco seasoning mix, ranch dressing mix, undrained corn, undrained tomatoes, beans, onion, celery, picante sauce, chili powder, garlic powder, salt, pepper, cumin and 3 tablespoons of the cilantro and mix well. Bring to a simmer. Cook for 1 to 1½ hours. Ladle into soup bowls. Sprinkle with the remaining cilantro and Cheddar cheese. Serve with tortilla chips.

YIELD: 6 SERVINGS

HOBERT HOGGARD
STATION 35

Station 26, located in southeast Houston between Gulfgate Mall and William P. Hobby Airport, serves many of Houston's petroleum plants, the airport, and several residential communities. They "run" with Stations 29, 35, 36, 40, and 46.

Chicken Soup for the Hungry Soul

4 CHICKENS	2 (8-OUNCE) CANS MUSHROOMS
1/2 BUNCH PARSLEY, CHOPPED	1/2 BUNCH PARSLEY, CHOPPED
2 LARGE ONIONS, CHOPPED	2 (16-OUNCE) PACKAGES FROZEN
SALT AND PEPPER TO TASTE	MIXED VEGETABLES
GARLIC TO TASTE	2 POUNDS RIGATONI PASTA
1 BUNCH CELERY, CHOPPED	FRESHLY GRATED PARMESAN
1 LARGE PACKAGE CARROTS,	CHEESE
CUT INTO 1-INCH PIECES	

Place the chickens, 1/2 bunch parsley and onions in a large pot. Add enough water to cover. Season with salt, pepper and garlic. Bring to a boil. Reduce the heat. Simmer for 45 minutes or until chickens are tender. Drain, reserving the broth. Remove the meat from the chickens, discarding the skin and bones. Cut the chicken into bite-size pieces. Strain the reserved broth.

Cook the celery, carrots and mushrooms in a saucepan until tender. Combine the reserved strained broth, chicken, carrot mixture, 1/2 bunch parsley and mixed vegetables in a large pot. Cook until heated through.

Cook the pasta using the package directions; drain. Stir into the chicken soup. Ladle into soup bowls. Serve with freshly grated Parmesan cheese.

NOTE: I got nominated to cook about 10 years ago and have been doing it ever since. I usually save this recipe for the colder months, although in Houston, we are lucky to get a full month of cold weather.

YIELD: 10 TO 12 SERVINGS

CLYDE GORDON
STATION 26

Chicken Noodle Soup

2 (15-OUNCE) CANS CHICKEN
    BROTH
½ CUP WATER
8 OUNCES CHICKEN TENDERS
½ CUP CHOPPED ONION
1 CUP SLICED CARROTS
1 CUP SLICED CELERY

1 CUP SLICED ZUCCHINI
1 CUP SLICED MUSHROOMS
⅔ CUP BROKEN EGG NOODLES
¼ CUP CHOPPED FRESH
    PARSLEY
SALT AND PEPPER TO TASTE

Bring the chicken broth and water to a boil in a saucepan over medium heat. Add the chicken tenders and stir. Remove from the heat. Let stand, covered, for 10 minutes. Remove the chicken tenders with a slotted spoon and set aside to cool.

Add the onion, carrots and celery to the broth. Bring to a boil. Reduce the heat and simmer for 10 minutes or until the vegetables are tender. Add the zucchini, mushrooms and noodles. Cook for 5 minutes.

Shred the chicken tenders. Stir into the broth mixture. Cook until heated through, adding additional water for thinner soup. Stir in the parsley. Season with salt and pepper.

You may substitute reduced-sodium chicken broth for the chicken broth.

YIELD: 4 SERVINGS

MICHAEL S. PLUMMER
FIRE ALARM

Deer Hunting

A rookie, a captain, and a chief went hunting. The weather was miserable, and they didn't see any deer all day. They came across an old shack and went inside to play poker. After losing a couple of hands, the captain threw down his cards and said, "That does it! I am going out to get me a deer." Fifteen minutes later he came back with a nice 4-point buck. The rookie and chief asked, "How did you get that?" The captain replied, "I walked out fifty feet, followed some tracks, and shot this buck." The chief then said, "I've had enough of this. I am going to get my deer." He came back a half hour later with a 6-point buck. The rookie asked, "How did you get that?" The chief replied, "I walked out a hundred feet, followed some tracks, and shot this buck." The rookie, not wanting to be outdone, said, "I am out of here; I am going to bag the biggest buck of the day." He came back an hour later, all mangled up and bloody. The chief and captain asked, "What happened to you?" The rookie replied, "I walked out there five hundred feet, followed some tracks, and got hit by a train."

Tortilla Soup

3 OR 4 CORN TORTILLAS
VEGETABLE OIL FOR FRYING
2 TABLESPOONS VEGETABLE OIL
1/3 CUP CHOPPED ONION
1 (4-OUNCE) CAN CHOPPED GREEN CHILES
4 CUPS CHICKEN BROTH
1 CUP SHREDDED CHICKEN
SALT TO TASTE
1 (10-OUNCE) CAN TOMATOES WITH GREEN CHILES
1 TABLESPOON LIME JUICE
1 CUP SHREDDED CHEDDAR CHEESE

Cut the tortillas into wedges. Fry in hot oil until crisp. Set on paper towels to drain.

Heat 2 tablespoons oil in a large skillet. Add the onion. Sauté until tender. Stir in the green chiles, chicken broth, chicken, salt and tomatoes. Cover and bring to a simmer. Cook for 20 minutes. Stir in the lime juice. Ladle into soup bowls. Add the tortilla wedges to the soup. Sprinkle with the Cheddar cheese.

YIELD: 4 SERVINGS

ROBERT HOGGARD
STATION 35

Broccoli Cheese Soup

1 BUNCH BROCCOLI, CUT INTO
    BITE-SIZE PIECES
1 CUP WATER
1/4 CUP (1/2 STICK) BUTTER
SALT AND PEPPER TO TASTE

1 (10-OUNCE) CAN CHEDDAR
    CHEESE SOUP
1 1/2 CUPS CUBED VELVEETA
    CHEESE
2 CUPS (ABOUT) MILK

Bring enough water to cover the broccoli to a boil in a saucepan. Add the broccoli. Cook until tender-crisp; drain. Combine the broccoli, 1 cup water, butter, salt, pepper, soup, Velveeta cheese and enough milk to make of the desired consistency in a saucepan. Cook over low heat until the cheese is melted, stirring constantly.

YIELD: 4 SERVINGS

ANDY COE
STATION 16

Tasty Tomato Soup

2 GARLIC CLOVES, MINCED
1 CUP (2 STICKS) BUTTER,
    MELTED
6 SLICES WHITE BREAD, CUBED
3 TABLESPOONS BUTTER
2 TABLESPOONS FLOUR
1 TEASPOON SALT, OR TO TASTE

1/2 TEASPOON PEPPER
2 CUPS STRAINED COOKED
    TOMATOES
1/4 TEASPOON EACH BAKING
    SODA, SALT AND PEPPER
1 CUP MILK

Combine the garlic, 1 cup butter and bread in a large bowl. Arrange in a thin layer on a baking sheet. Bake at 350 degrees until crisp, turning every 5 minutes.

Melt 3 tablespoons butter in a saucepan. Stir in the flour, 1 teaspoon salt and 1/2 teaspoon pepper. Remove from the heat. Add the tomatoes and mix well. Cook for 5 minutes. Stir in the baking soda, 1/4 teaspoon salt and 1/4 teaspoon pepper. Stir in the milk. Bring to a boil. Ladle into bowls. Serve with the croutons.

YIELD: 2 SERVINGS

LISA HAVLICE
STATION 18

Hogs House Chicken and Sausage Gumbo

4 TO 6 CUPS CHICKEN BROTH
1/2 CUP VEGETABLE OIL
1/2 CUP FLOUR
1 ONION, CHOPPED
1 BELL PEPPER, CHOPPED
1 RIB CELERY, CHOPPED
1 POUND OKRA, SLICED
3 GARLIC CLOVES, CHOPPED
2 (14-OUNCE) CANS STEWED
    TOMATOES, SLICED
1 (3- TO 4-POUND) CHICKEN,
    COOKED, BONED, CUT INTO
    BITE-SIZE PIECES
2 POUNDS POLSKA KIELBASA
    SAUSAGE, SLICED
1 TEASPOON TONY CHACHERE'S
    ORIGINAL SEASONING
SALT AND PEPPER TO TASTE
1 TABLESPOON FILÉ POWDER

Bring the chicken broth to a boil in a large pot. Heat the oil in a large skillet. Add the flour. Cook until medium to dark brown, stirring constantly. Stir a small amount of the boiling chicken broth into the roux. Stir the roux mixture into the boiling chicken broth.

Add the onion, bell pepper, celery, okra, garlic and tomatoes to the broth mixture. Cook for 5 minutes. Stir in the chicken, sausage, Cajun seasoning, salt, pepper and filé powder. Cook for 10 to 15 minutes.

You may substitute crab, oysters and shrimp for the chicken and sausage.

YIELD: 10 TO 12 SERVINGS

ROBERT HOGGARD
STATION 35

"Batman's" Uptown Throwdown Seafood Gumbo

1 (5-POUND) CHICKEN, CUT UP
GARLIC POWDER TO TASTE
ONION POWDER TO TASTE
PEPPER TO TASTE
3 POUNDS HOT LINKS, SLICED
5 QUARTS WATER
6 TABLESPOONS TONY CHACHERE'S ORIGINAL SEASONING
2 ONIONS, CHOPPED
2 RIBS CELERY, CHOPPED
2 BELL PEPPERS, CHOPPED
4 BAY LEAVES
2 BUNCHES GREEN ONIONS, CHOPPED
4 GARLIC CLOVES, MINCED
1 CUP CHOPPED PARSLEY

2 POUNDS SMOKED TURKEY NECKS, CUT UP
4 CUPS CHICKEN STOCK
2 (15-OUNCE) CANS TOMATO SAUCE
2 (10-OUNCE) CANS TOMATOES WITH GREEN CHILES, CHOPPED
4 CUPS "BATMAN'S" FAT-FREE CHOLESTEROL-FREE ROUX (AT RIGHT)
2 POUNDS OKRA, CHOPPED
5 POUNDS MEDIUM OR LARGE SHRIMP, PEELED, DEVEINED
4 POUNDS CRABS, CLEANED, SPLIT
2 POUNDS OYSTERS (OPTIONAL)
1 BAG CRAB BOIL

Season the chicken with the garlic powder, onion powder and pepper. Arrange chicken pieces in a single layer on a baking sheet. Bake at 400 degrees for 1 hour.

Combine the hot links with enough water to cover. Bring to a boil. Boil until cooked through; drain. Combine 5 quarts water and the next 8 ingredients in a large pot. Bring to a boil. Add the hot links, smoked turkey, baked chicken, chicken stock, tomato sauce and tomatoes and mix well. Cook for 25 to 30 minutes.

Bring the gumbo to a boil. Stir in the roux. Reduce the heat. Simmer for 15 minutes, stirring occasionally. Stir in the okra. Simmer for 10 to 15 minutes. Add the shrimp, crabs, oysters and crab boil. Simmer for 15 to 25 minutes; the longer the crab boil bag is in the gumbo the spicier it will be. Remove the crab boil and bay leaves. Adjust the seasonings. Serve over hot cooked rice.

YIELD: 25 TO 30

LARY D. BATISTE
STATION 3

"Batman's" Fat-Free Cholesterol-Free Roux

Spray a cast-iron skillet generously with nonstick cooking spray. Spread 4 cups flour evenly over the bottom of the skillet. Bake at 400 degrees until golden to dark brown, stirring every 12 to 15 minutes. Store in the refrigerator until ready to use.

One helping of this gumbo is not nearly enough. Anyone eating this dish will be guaranteed to come back for second and third helpings. You won't eat until you get full; you'll eat until you get tired. This dish is a low-fat gumbo because of the fat-free roux.

Fire Station 13 or "Lucky 13" serves the northwest residential community of Oak Forest. Opened in 1956, Station 13 houses an engine and ambulance.

Award-Winning Spicy Ricey Bacon Salad

1 (10-OUNCE) PACKAGE FROZEN
  PEAS WITH PEARL ONIONS,
  PARTIALLY THAWED
6 SLICES BACON
3 CUPS COOKED RICE, COOLED
5 GREEN ONIONS, THINLY SLICED
2 RIBS CELERY, CHOPPED

2 TO 3 TABLESPOONS
  MAYONNAISE, OR TO TASTE
2 TABLESPOONS PICANTE SAUCE,
  OR TO TASTE
¼ TEASPOON SALT
¼ TEASPOON PEPPER

Bring enough water to cover the peas to a boil in a saucepan. Add the peas. Cook until warm; drain. Fry the bacon in a skillet until crisp; drain. Crumble the bacon.

Combine the rice, peas, bacon, green onions, celery, mayonnaise, picante sauce, salt and pepper in a bowl and mix well.

Serve warm or cooled.

NOTE: This recipe was featured in the USA Rice Council's *Greatest Firehouse Chefs Cookbook* and the *Houston Chronicle*. Al Kiel has since retired from HFD. He says, "We decide what to cook by what is on sale. My favorite cooking tip is 'Use hot sauce!'"

YIELD: 8 SERVINGS

AL KIEL
RETIRED

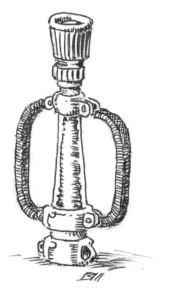

Turkey Taco Salad

1 LARGE ONION, CHOPPED

5 POUNDS GROUND TURKEY

2 TABLESPOONS DRIED OREGANO

½ CUP CHILI POWDER, OR TO
    TASTE

2 TEASPOONS CUMIN

3 (16-OUNCE) CANS KIDNEY
    BEANS, DRAINED, RINSED

3 (16-OUNCE) CANS PINTO BEANS,
    DRAINED, RINSED

3 (16-OUNCE) CANS DICED
    TOMATOES, DRAINED

2 (12-OUNCE) BAGS SALAD MIX

4 CUPS NONFAT MAYONNAISE

1 CUP PICANTE SAUCE

1 LARGE BAG TORTILLA CHIPS

4 CUPS SHREDDED CHEDDAR
    CHEESE

Cook the onion in a nonstick skillet over medium heat until tender. Add the turkey. Cook until the turkey is brown and crumbly, stirring constantly; drain. Stir in the oregano, chili powder and cumin. Cook for 1 minute.

Combine the kidney beans, pinto beans and tomatoes in a large bowl and mix well. Add the turkey mixture and mix well. Add the salad mix and toss to combine.

Combine the mayonnaise and picante sauce in a bowl and mix well. Add to the salad and toss to coat. Serve immediately with the tortilla chips and Cheddar cheese.

YIELD: 15 TO 20 SERVINGS

BUTCH HAYES
STATION 22

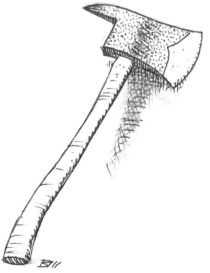

Antipasto Salad

1 (12-OUNCE) PACKAGE SALAD
    TWIRL PASTA, COOKED,
    DRAINED
1 (4-OUNCE) CAN BLACK OLIVES,
    DRAINED
1 (4-OUNCE) CAN SLICED
    MUSHROOMS, DRAINED, OR
    1 CUP SLICED FRESH
    MUSHROOMS
1 (8-OUNCE) CAN ARTICHOKE
    HEARTS, DRAINED, CUT INTO
    QUARTERS
1 BELL PEPPER, THINLY SLICED

½ CUP THINLY SLICED PURPLE
    ONION
¾ CUP THINLY SLICED RADISHES
½ CUP COARSELY GRATED
    CARROTS
¾ CUP JULIENNED ZUCCHINI
1 TEASPOON OREGANO
½ TEASPOON SALT
¾ TEASPOON PEPPER
1 (11-OUNCE) BOTTLE ITALIAN
    SALAD DRESSING
GRATED PARMESAN CHEESE

Combine the pasta, olives, mushrooms, artichoke hearts, bell pepper, onion, radishes, carrots and zucchini in a large bowl and mix well. Add the oregano, salt, pepper and salad dressing and toss to combine.

Chill, covered, for 2½ hours or longer; for maximum flavor refrigerate for 6 to 8 hours. Sprinkle with Parmesan cheese and serve.

You may substitute tomatoes, squash, cucumbers, celery, broccoli, cauliflower or any other seasonal vegetable for any vegetable in the recipe. You may also add your favorite meat, such as pepperoni, ham, grilled chicken or salami, to make a main dish salad.

NOTE: We like this salad in the summer because we make it in the morning and it's ready by suppertime.

YIELD: 6 SERVINGS

NANCY KAMMAN
STATION 7

Apple Coleslaw

1 CUP BUTTERMILK

½ CUP REDUCED-FAT
    MAYONNAISE

2 TABLESPOONS RICE WINE
    VINEGAR

1 TABLESPOON DIJON MUSTARD

2 TEASPOONS SUGAR

¼ TO ½ TEASPOON SALT

2 GREEN APPLES, SUCH AS PIPPIN
    OR GRANNY SMITH, PEELED,
    CHOPPED

1 TABLESPOON RICE WINE
    VINEGAR

1 CUP SHREDDED CARROTS

½ CUP FINELY CHOPPED
    GREEN ONIONS

2 CUPS CHOPPED GREEN
    CABBAGE

2 CUPS CHOPPED RED CABBAGE

Combine the buttermilk, mayonnaise, 2 tablespoons rice wine vinegar, mustard, sugar and salt in a large bowl and mix well.

Combine the apples and 1 tablespoon rice wine vinegar in a bowl and toss to coat; drain. Add to the buttermilk mixture. Toss to coat the apple pieces.

Add the carrots, green onions and cabbage to the buttermilk mixture; do not mix. Chill, covered, until ready to serve. Toss to coat the vegetables with the buttermilk mixture. Serve immediately.

YIELD: 4 SERVINGS

MICHAEL S. PLUMMER
FIRE ALARM

Austin's Pasta Salad

2 (16-OUNCE) PACKAGES ROTINI	SALT AND PEPPER TO TASTE
2 (16-OUNCE) PACKAGES FROZEN	GARLIC TO TASTE
MIXED VEGETABLES	GRATED PARMESAN CHEESE
1 (16-OUNCE) BOTTLE ITALIAN	
SALAD DRESSING	

Cook the rotini using the package directions; drain. Cook the vegetables using the package directions; drain.

Combine the pasta, vegetables and 1/2 of the salad dressing in a large bowl and mix well. Season with salt, pepper and garlic. Refrigerate, covered, until chilled.

Pour the remaining 1/2 bottle of salad dressing over the salad and mix well. Sprinkle with Parmesan cheese.

YIELD: 8 SERVINGS
HOBERT HOGGARD
STATION 16

Bill's Sweet Pea Salad

6 (15-OUNCE) CANS SWEET PEAS,	6 HARD-COOKED EGGS, FINELY
DRAINED	CHOPPED
1/2 ONION, MINCED	1 1/2 CUPS SALAD DRESSING
3/4 CUP CHOPPED BREAD-AND-	SALT AND PEPPER TO TASTE
BUTTER PICKLES	GARLIC POWDER TO TASTE
3 RIBS CELERY, CHOPPED	
1/2 CUP SHREDDED CHEDDAR	
CHEESE	

Combine the peas, onion, pickles, celery, cheese, eggs and salad dressing in a large bowl and mix well. Season with salt, pepper and garlic powder.

Chill, covered, for 3 hours.

YIELD: 8 TO 10 SERVINGS
HOBERT HOGGARD
STATION 16

Artichoke Casserole

2 (10-OUNCE) PACKAGES FROZEN CHOPPED SPINACH
½ CUP FINELY CHOPPED ONION
½ CUP (1 STICK) BUTTER
2 CUPS SOUR CREAM
½ CUP (OR MORE) GRATED PARMESAN CHEESE
1 (14-OUNCE) CAN ARTICHOKES, CHOPPED
SALT AND PEPPER TO TASTE
GRATED PARMESAN CHEESE

Cook the spinach using the package directions; drain. Sauté the onion in the butter in a skillet. Combine the cooked spinach, onion and butter, sour cream, ½ cup Parmesan cheese and artichokes in a bowl and mix well. Season with salt and pepper.

Spoon the artichoke mixture into a greased 2-quart baking dish. Sprinkle additional Parmesan cheese over the top. Bake at 350 degrees for 25 minutes.

YIELD: 6 TO 8 SERVINGS

KENNY BOLES
STATION 103

Number 1

One recipe that is a part of every fire station's menu—at least it used to be—was what was simply known as, "Number 1." You could fill-in at another station and ask what's for dinner and if they said "Number 1," you knew exactly what they were talking about. It kind of developed into the "We can't decide on anything else so we're having Number 1" idea. Number 1 is hamburger patties, seasoned with everything from Cajun seasoning to onion soup mix, browned in a pan and smothered in gravy (I like mushroom gravy). Served over mashed potatoes, with a vegetable on the side, it carries enough weight to fill up even the hungriest firefighters. P.S. Don't forget the buttered bread.

Old-Fashioned Baked Beans

3 CUPS DRIED NAVY BEANS
³/4 CUP CHILI SAUCE
1¹/2 TEASPOONS CIDER VINEGAR
2 ONIONS, THINLY SLICED

³/4 TEASPOON DRY MUSTARD
¹/2 CUP DARK MOLASSES
3 CUPS WATER

Sort and rinse the beans. Combine the beans with enough water to cover in a stockpot. Bring to a boil. Boil for 2 minutes. Remove from the heat. Let stand for 1 hour; drain.

Combine the beans, chili sauce, cider vinegar, onions, mustard, molasses and 3 cups water in a baking dish and mix well. Bake, covered, at 300 degrees for 5 hours, adding additional water if the beans begin to dry out.

YIELD: 8 SERVINGS

JIM "BIG DOG" HARLING
VAL JAHNKE TRAINING ACADEMY

Drunken "Borracho" Beans

2 CUPS DRIED BEANS
4 CUPS WATER
2 GARLIC CLOVES, CHOPPED
2 TEASPOONS SALT (OPTIONAL)
16 OUNCES BACON, CHOPPED
1 ONION, CHOPPED

1 TOMATO, CHOPPED
1 JALAPEÑO CHILE, CHOPPED
1 CUP CHOPPED CILANTRO
1 (12-OUNCE) CAN BEER
  (OPTIONAL)

Sort and rinse the beans. Bring the water to a boil in a saucepan. Add the beans, garlic and salt. Reduce the heat to medium. Cook for 15 minutes. Add the bacon. Cook until the beans are tender. Add the onion, tomato, chile and cilantro and mix well. Stir in the beer. Simmer, covered, until the onion is tender.

YIELD: 4 TO 6 SERVINGS

ANN MARIE RODRIGUEZ
ADMINISTRATION

Firehouse Code 3 Homemade Quick Beans

5 (16-OUNCE) CANS PINTO BEANS, DRAINED

1 (10-OUNCE) CAN TOMATOES WITH GREEN CHILES

1 (14-OUNCE) CAN WHOLE PEELED TOMATOES, CHOPPED

2 SMALL TOMATOES, CHOPPED

⅔ CUP WORCESTERSHIRE SAUCE

2 TABLESPOONS (HEAPING) SPICY BROWN MUSTARD

1 TABLESPOON (HEAPING) DARK BROWN SUGAR

1 TEASPOON MINCED GARLIC

1 MEDIUM RED ONION, CHOPPED

1 BUNCH CILANTRO, CHOPPED

1 TABLESPOON PEPPER

1 TABLESPOON (HEAPING) TONY CHACHERE'S ORIGINAL SEASONING

CILANTRO TO TASTE

Combine the beans, tomatoes, Worcestershire sauce, mustard, brown sugar, garlic, onion, 1 bunch cilantro, pepper and Tony Chachere's Original Seasoning in a large pot and mix well. Cook until heated through, stirring occasionally.

Sprinkle with additional chopped fresh cilantro to serve.

YIELD: 15 TO 20 SERVINGS

NICK GUILLEN
STATION 54

ARFF Team

The Houston Fire Department Aircraft Rescue Firefighting Team (ARFF) provides a safe exit path and timely rescue of aircraft crash victims. All members of the ARFF team are certified EMTs and respond to air crash entrapments and large hydrocarbon fuel fires. Additionally, they assist major carriers in extinguisher and rescue classes.

Mean Green Beans

16 OUNCES BACON, CHOPPED
4 OUNCES FRESH MUSHROOMS, SLICED
1 LARGE ONION, CHOPPED

6 (15-OUNCE) CANS GREEN BEANS, DRAINED
SALT AND PEPPER TO TASTE

Cook the bacon in a skillet until almost crisp. Add the mushrooms and onion. Cook until the bacon is crisp and the onion is tender. Add the green beans and mix well. Season with salt and pepper. Cook over medium-low heat for 30 minutes or until heated through, stirring occasionally.

YIELD: 15 TO 18 SERVINGS

DANIEL P. MATT
STATION 28

Sweet-and-Sour Green Beans

2 (16-OUNCE) CANS GREEN BEANS, DRAINED
RED ONION TO TASTE, THINLY SLICED
1/2 CUP VINEGAR

1/2 CUP SUGAR
1/4 CUP WATER
2 TABLESPOONS VEGETABLE OIL
1/2 TEASPOON MSG (OPTIONAL)
PEPPER TO TASTE

Alternate layers of the green beans and red onion in a baking dish until the green beans and onion are used.

Combine the vinegar, sugar and water in a small saucepan. Bring to a boil. Stir in the oil, MSG and pepper and mix well. Pour over the layers of green beans and onion.

Refrigerate, covered, until chilled.

YIELD: 8 SERVINGS

BEN BRYMER
STATION 64

Broccoli Cheese Casserole

½ CUP (1 STICK) MARGARINE
1 LARGE ONION, CHOPPED
1 (10-OUNCE) PACKAGE FROZEN
    CHOPPED BROCCOLI

1 (10-OUNCE) CAN CREAM OF
    MUSHROOM SOUP
1 (8-OUNCE) JAR CHEEZ WHIZ
1 SOUP CAN INSTANT RICE

Heat the margarine in a saucepan until melted. Add the onion. Cook until tender, stirring frequently. Add the broccoli, soup, Cheez Whiz and rice and mix well.

Spoon the broccoli mixture into a baking pan. Bake at 350 degrees for 45 minutes or until the top is lightly browned.

YIELD: 6 SERVINGS

STEVE BRADFORD
STATION 2

Meaux Chow

3 (16-OUNCE) CANS WHOLE
    KERNEL CORN
16 OUNCES CREAM CHEESE

3 JALAPEÑO CHILES, SEEDED,
    FINELY CHOPPED

Combine the corn and cream cheese in a saucepan. Cook until the cream cheese begins to melt. Add the jalapeño chiles. Cook until the cream cheese is melted, stirring frequently.

YIELD: 10 TO 12 SERVINGS

KEITH BOBBITT
STATION 11

Technical Rescue Team

The Houston Fire Department Technical Rescue Team of forty members is a highly specialized team that responds to some of the most unusual and out-of-the-ordinary rescues. Responses include rescues in swift water in some of Houston's heavy torrential rains and flooding. They conduct high-angle or rope rescues as well as rescues from trenches, tunnels, confined spaces, cave-ins, and structural collapses.

Tater Tot Casserole

2 POUNDS GROUND TURKEY
1 ONION, CHOPPED
TONY CHACHERE'S ORIGINAL SEASONING
2 (10-OUNCE) CANS CREAM OF CHICKEN SOUP
2 (10-OUNCE) CANS CREAM OF CELERY SOUP
¼ CUP MILK
1 (32-OUNCE) PACKAGE TATER TOTS

Brown the turkey with the onion in a skillet, stirring until the turkey is crumbly; drain. Season with Tony Chachere's Original Seasoning. Arrange over the bottom of a 9×13-inch baking dish.

Combine the chicken soup and celery soup in a bowl and mix well. Stir in the milk. Pour over the turkey mixture, covering the entire layer. Poke the soup mixture into the turkey mixture; do not mix. Cover the top with the Tater Tots.

Bake at 400 degrees for 30 to 45 minutes or until hot and bubbly and Tater Tots are cooked through.

YIELD: 6 TO 8 SERVINGS

JEFF BOLES
STATION 37

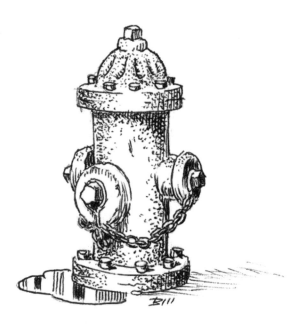

SIDE DISHES

Firehouse Twice-Baked Potatoes

5 POUNDS POTATOES
2 POUNDS BACON
1 BUNCH GREEN ONIONS

1 MEDIUM YELLOW ONION
16 OUNCES VELVEETA CHEESE
BUTTER TO TASTE

Peel the potatoes and dice. Combine the potatoes with enough water to cover in a large saucepan. Bring to a boil. Boil until tender; drain.

Cut the bacon into bite size pieces. Cook in a skillet until crisp; drain. Chop the green onions and yellow onion. Cut the Velveeta cheese into cubes.

Combine the potatoes, bacon, green onions, yellow onion, cheese and butter in a large ovenproof pot and mix well. Mash to the desired consistency. Bake, covered, at 375 degrees for 45 to 60 minutes or until brown on top and heated through.

YIELD: 15 TO 20 SERVINGS

ENNIO PONTE
STATION 25

Grilled Squash

4 MEDIUM YELLOW SQUASH
OLIVE OIL
BUTTER, SOFTENED
TOMATOES

ONION
OREGANO TO TASTE
SALT AND PEPPER TO TASTE

Cut the squash into halves lengthwise. Brush with olive oil. Spread butter over the squash. Place cut side up on a piece of foil.

Thinly slice the tomatoes and onion. Arrange over the squash. Sprinkle with oregano, salt and pepper. Seal the foil.

Place on a grill over hot coals. Grill until squash is tender.

YIELD: 8 SERVINGS

MICHAEL R. GANN
RETIRED

In 1977, Houston annexed Clear Lake City, Texas, home to NASA/Johnson Space Center, midway between Houston and Galveston Island. Station 72 opened in April 1978 on the Johnson Space Center base. In 1999, HFD relocated to a fire station off the base on Space Center Boulevard. Though they still respond to NASA, Space Center Operations is one of four stations (Fire Stations 71, 72, and 94) serving an estimated population of 54,000 in Clear Lake City.

Zucchini Italiano

1 POUND FRESH ZUCCHINI	½ TEASPOON SALT
1 MEDIUM ONION, SLICED	2 TABLESPOONS GRATED
1 TABLESPOON VEGETABLE OIL	PARMESAN CHEESE

Cut the zucchini into thin slices. Sauté the onion in the oil in a skillet until golden brown. Add the zucchini. Sprinkle with the salt. Cook, covered, for 5 minutes or until tender-crisp. Sprinkle with the cheese.

YIELD: 4 SERVINGS

LYDIA HENN
STAFF SERVICES

Sweet Potato Casserole

3 CUPS MASHED COOKED SWEET POTATOES, ABOUT 6 TO 7 SWEET POTATOES	½ CUP MILK
	1½ TEASPOONS VANILLA EXTRACT
½ CUP SUGAR	½ CUP PACKED BROWN SUGAR
½ TEASPOON SALT	⅓ CUP FLOUR
2 EGGS, BEATEN	1 CUP FINELY CHOPPED PECANS
¼ CUP (½ STICK) BUTTER OR MARGARINE, SOFTENED	3 TABLESPOONS BUTTER OR MARGARINE, MELTED

Combine the sweet potatoes, sugar, salt, eggs, ¼ cup butter, milk and vanilla in a bowl and mix well. Spoon into a 2-quart baking dish.

Combine the brown sugar, flour, pecans and 3 tablespoons butter in a bowl and mix well. Sprinkle over the top of the sweet potato mixture.

Bake at 350 degrees for 35 to 40 minutes. You may freeze the casserole before baking.

YIELD: 8 TO 10 SERVINGS

LINDA EVERS TRIPPODO
DAUGHTER OF JOSEPH EVERS

Sweet, Sweet Potatoes, Sweet

4 LARGE SWEET POTATOES
BUTTER, SLICED
BROWN SUGAR

CINNAMON
MINIATURE MARSHMALLOWS

Combine the sweet potatoes with enough water to cover in a large saucepan. Bring to a boil. Boil until tender; drain. Peel and cut each sweet potato into 3 or 4 lengthwise slices. Arrange the slices over the bottom of a 9×13-inch baking pan.

Place butter over the sweet potatoes. Sprinkle brown sugar and cinnamon over the sweet potatoes. Cover with marshmallows. Bake at 350 degrees until the marshmallows are toasted.

NOTE: I learned how to cook at the fire station about 13 years ago. I had to learn since all the others were too lazy to cook. When I get stuck, I rely on my mom Joan, who is always there to help.

YIELD: 8 TO 10 SERVINGS

DANIEL P. MATT
STATION 28

Stuffed Sweet Potatoes

2 MEDIUM SWEET POTATOES
½ CUP RAISINS
1 CUP CRUSHED PINEAPPLE
1 TEASPOON CINNAMON

1 CUP PACKED BROWN SUGAR
¼ CUP (½ STICK) MARGARINE,
  SOFTENED

Place the sweet potatoes on a baking sheet. Bake at 300 degrees until syrup begins to seep from the peel. Slice off the tops of the sweet potatoes. Scoop out the pulp, reserving the shells. Combine the pulp with the remaining ingredients in a bowl and mix well. Spoon into the reserved sweet potato shells.

Place the stuffed sweet potatoes on the baking sheet. Bake for 45 minutes or until the brown sugar is melted and the raisins are plump. Omit the margarine for more healthful stuffed sweet potatoes.

YIELD: 4 SERVINGS

BILLY HUNT
STATION 8

Fire Station 28

Eating 'on the run' is typical at Fire Station 28, one of the busiest stations in southwest Houston. The firefighters cook slowly, because at any time, they may have to go. To guarantee a hot meal, they even installed a second oven. "We never know when we are coming back," says Firefighter Daniel Matt, head cook on the B shift. Ranked consistently as one of the top three busiest stations, the "Richmond Knights" respond to Houston's famous Richmond Strip, lined with businesses, nightclubs, and restaurants.

Arroz—Del Rio Grande

VEGETABLE OIL

1½ CUPS RICE

1 MEDIUM ONION, CHOPPED

½-INCH-WIDE SLICE BELL
  PEPPER, CHOPPED

1 GARLIC CLOVE, MINCED

½ (16-OUNCE) CAN MEXICAN-
  STYLE TOMATOES, CHOPPED

3 CUPS WATER

SALT TO TASTE

¼ TEASPOON PEPPER

⅛ TEASPOON CUMIN, GROUND

1 CHICKEN BOUILLON CUBE,
  CRUSHED

1 (8-OUNCE) CAN TOMATO SAUCE

7 SPRIGS OF CILANTRO, LEAVES
  CHOPPED

Pour enough oil in a skillet to cover the bottom. Heat over medium heat. Add the rice, onion, bell pepper and garlic. Cook until the rice is golden brown, stirring constantly. Stir in the undrained tomatoes. Add the water, salt, pepper, cumin, bouillon granules and tomato sauce and mix well. Bring to a simmer. Simmer for 10 minutes. Stir in the cilantro.

Simmer for 20 minutes or until the liquid is reduced to half the height of the rice; do not stir. Add an additional 1 cup of water if rice is not tender and simmer until liquid is reduced to half the height of the rice; do not stir.

YIELD: 4 TO 6 SERVINGS

DANIEL SALAZAR
COMMUNITY RELATIONS

SIDE DISHES

Hot Dirty Rice

10 CHICKEN GIZZARDS
10 CHICKEN NECKS
10 CHICKEN LIVERS
10 CHICKEN HEARTS
8 CUPS WATER
4 POUNDS HOT SAUSAGE
2 LARGE YELLOW ONIONS,
   MINCED

1 LARGE BELL PEPPER, MINCED
4 RIBS CELERY, MINCED
1 BUNCH GREEN ONIONS, MINCED
1 CUP CHOPPED HAM
2 TABLESPOONS DRIED PARSLEY
½ CUP (1 STICK) BUTTER
SALT TO TASTE
2 POUNDS COOKED RICE

Combine the chicken gizzards, necks, livers and hearts with the water in a large saucepan. Bring to a boil. Boil until cooked through. Drain, reserving the liquid. Chop the gizzards, livers and hearts. Discard the necks.

Cook the sausage in a skillet, stirring until crumbly. Drain, reserving the drippings. Cook the yellow onions, bell pepper and celery in 3 tablespoons of the reserved sausage drippings in a skillet for 20 minutes, stirring frequently. Add the green onions. Cook for 10 minutes, stirring frequently.

Add the gizzards, livers, hearts, ham, sausage, parsley and butter to the vegetable mixture and mix well. Add enough of the reserved liquid to make a moist mixture. Season with salt. Simmer for 15 minutes. Fold in the rice. Serve immediately or place in a double boiler to keep warm.

YIELD: 15 SERVINGS

AL YOUNG
STATION 69

Hot Rice with Spinach

2 TABLESPOONS BUTTER
1 GARLIC CLOVE, MINCED
1 JALAPEÑO CHILE,
   FINELY CHOPPED
1/4 CUP FINELY CHOPPED ONION

1/4 CUP FINELY CHOPPED FRESH
   SPINACH
2 CUPS WHITE RICE
4 CUPS WATER
SALT TO TASTE

Heat the butter in a saucepan over medium heat until melted. Add the garlic, jalapeño chile and onion. Sauté for 1 minute. Add the spinach. Sauté for 1 minute.

Stir the rice into the vegetable mixture. Increase the heat to high. Pour in the water. Bring to a boil. Reduce the heat to low. Cook, covered, for 15 minutes. Season with salt.

YIELD: 4 SERVINGS

AURORA CARRASCO
HFD FITNESS CENTER

Corn Bread Stuffing

3 (7-OUNCE) PACKAGES CORN
   BREAD MIX
1 (6-OUNCE) PACKAGE
   HERB-SEASONED
   STUFFING MIX
1/2 CUP CHOPPED ONION

2 CUPS CHOPPED CELERY
BUTTER
SALT AND PEPPER TO TASTE
4 OR 5 (10-OUNCE) CANS
   CHICKEN BROTH
6 EGGS

Prepare the corn bread using the package directions. Let stand until cool. Crumble into a large bowl. Add the stuffing mix.

Sauté the onion and celery in a small amount of butter in a skillet until tender. Season with salt and pepper. Add to the corn bread mixture and mix well. Add enough broth to make a very moist mixture, adding water if needed. You may refrigerate the mixture, covered, at this point.

Add the eggs and mix well. Spoon into a greased baking pan. Bake at 350 degrees for 1 hour.

YIELD: 8 TO 10 SERVINGS

SCOTT S. GRANT
STATION 78

Italian Stuffing

1½ CUPS BREAD CRUMBS
1 CUP GRATED ROMANO CHEESE
1 LARGE ONION, CHOPPED
4 GARLIC CLOVES, MINCED
4 TEASPOONS SALT
1 TABLESPOON PEPPER
4 EGGS

1 TABLESPOON DRIED PARSLEY,
 OR CHOPPED LEAVES OF 3 OR
 4 STEMS FRESH PARSLEY
1 TABLESPOON DRIED
 PEPPERMINT, OR 1 TEASPOON
 FRESH PEPPERMINT
1½ CUPS WATER

Combine the bread crumbs, cheese, onion, garlic, salt, pepper, eggs, parsley, peppermint and water in a large bowl and mix well. Spoon into a baking dish. Bake at 375 degrees for 30 to 40 minutes or until a knife inserted in the center comes out clean.

YIELD: 6 TO 8 SERVINGS   TERRY LITZINGER
                                       STATION 75

Spiced Cranberry Sauce

1 POUND CRANBERRIES
2 CUPS SUGAR
⅛ TEASPOON SALT
½ CUP WATER

½ TEASPOON ALLSPICE
½ TEASPOON CINNAMON
⅛ TEASPOON CLOVES
⅛ TEASPOON GINGER

Combine the cranberries, sugar, salt and water in a saucepan and stir to combine. Bring to a boil. Reduce the heat. Simmer for 8 minutes or until the cranberries burst. Remove from the heat.
Stir in the allspice, cinnamon, cloves and ginger. Let stand for 20 to 30 minutes. Chill, covered, in the refrigerator. The sauce will keep for up to 1 year.

YIELD: 16 SERVINGS   GABINO "GABE" CORTEZ
                                           ARSON

RED HOT MEATS

Built in 1968, northwest Houston's Station 62 has often been called the "Glass House" since it seems to have more glass than most every other fire station. This station serves the residential communities of Lazybrook and Timbergrove, numerous apartment complexes, a large industrial district, several high-rise buildings, and three major freeway intersections.

Michele Harris Salpicón

1 (3-POUND) BRISKET	1 (4-OUNCE) CAN CHIPOTLE
1 ONION, CUT INTO	CHILES
HALVES	1 ONION, CHOPPED
1 LARGE CARROT, CUT INTO	1 LARGE TOMATO, CHOPPED
QUARTERS	½ CUP CHOPPED FRESH
1 RIB CELERY, CUT INTO	CILANTRO
QUARTERS	¼ CUP LIGHT OLIVE OIL
2 GARLIC CLOVES	¼ CUP VINEGAR
½ CUP CHOPPED FRESH	8 OUNCES MONTEREY JACK
CILANTRO	CHEESE, CUT INTO ¼-INCH
1 (12-OUNCE) CAN WHOLE	CUBES
TOMATOES	2 LARGE AVOCADOS, CUT INTO
SALT AND PEPPER TO TASTE	LENGTHWISE SLICES

Place the brisket in a heavy ovenproof pot. Add enough water to cover the brisket. Add the onion halves, carrot, celery, garlic, ½ cup cilantro, whole tomatoes, salt and pepper. Cook at 325 degrees for 4 hours or until very tender. Remove the brisket and let stand until cooled. Shred and place in a large bowl.

Drain the chipotle chiles, reserving the liquid. Chop the chiles. Add the chopped chiles and reserved liquid to the brisket. Add the chopped onion, chopped tomato, ½ cup cilantro, olive oil and vinegar and mix well. Season with salt and pepper. Chill, covered, for 4 hours or longer.

Add the cheese to the brisket mixture and toss to mix. Spoon into a serving bowl. Garnish with the avocado slices. Serve with warm tortillas, pinto beans and guacamole or a tossed green salad.

Gringo Salpicón—Substitute one 4-ounce can chopped green chiles for half of the chipotle chiles. You may substitute chopped jalapeño chiles for the chipotle chiles.

Muy Gringo Salpicón—Substitute two 4-ounce cans chopped green chiles for the chipotle chiles.

NOTE: Served to the crew of Fire Station 62B under the false pretense of greatly enhancing one's employment opportunities. She married well and hasn't been seen since.

YIELD: 15 SERVINGS

HARVEY BIRDWELL
RETIRED

MEATS

Easy Brisket

ALL-PURPOSE SEASONING   1 MEDIUM BRISKET
POWDERED GARLIC

Rub a liberal amount of seasoning and garlic over the brisket. Chill, covered, for 8 to 12 hours.

Place on a grill over mesquite coals. Grill for 30 minutes on each side. Wrap fat side up in foil. Bake at 250 degrees for 2½ to 3 hours or until tender. Let stand until cooled. Cut into slices.

YIELD: VARIABLE   MICHAEL GANN
RETIRED

Cracked Pepper Tenderloin

⅔ CUP RHINE WINE   1½ TEASPOONS SALT
⅓ CUP OLIVE OIL   1 (3- TO 4-POUND) TENDERLOIN
1 SMALL ONION, CHOPPED   2 TABLESPOONS CRACKED
1 GARLIC CLOVE, MINCED   BLACK PEPPER

Combine the wine, olive oil, onion, garlic and salt in a bowl and mix well. Place the tenderloin in a sealable plastic bag. Pour the wine mixture over the tenderloin and seal the bag. Marinate for 6 to 12 hours in the refrigerator, turning several times. Drain the tenderloin and pat dry.

Roll the tenderloin in the pepper to coat. Bake in a baking pan at 425 degrees for 20 to 30 minutes or until a meat thermometer registers 120 degrees. Let stand for 5 to 6 minutes per pound. Cut into 1½-inch-thick slices.

YIELD: 8 TO 12 SERVINGS   GABINO "GABE" CORTEZ
ARSON

Pepper Steak

1 (5-POUND) ROUND STEAK
½ CUP SOY SAUCE
4 BELL PEPPERS, THINLY SLICED
2 MEDIUM ONIONS, THINLY
    SLICED
¼ CUP VEGETABLE OIL

2 BEEF BOUILLON CUBES
SALT AND PEPPER TO TASTE
MINCED GARLIC TO TASTE
3 TABLESPOONS CORNSTARCH
½ CUP COLD WATER

Cut the steak into thin slices. Place in a shallow dish. Pour the soy sauce over the steak, stirring to coat.

Place a vegetable steamer in a large saucepan. Add 1 inch of water. Cover and bring to a boil. Add the bell peppers and onions. Steam, covered, until the bell peppers are tender-crisp.

Drain the steak. Stir-fry in hot oil in a wok until brown. Add the bell pepper mixture, bouillon cubes, salt, pepper and garlic and mix well, adding water if the mixture is too dry. Combine the cornstarch and cold water in a small bowl and mix well. Stir into the steak mixture. Cook until the sauce is thickened. Serve over rice or pasta.

YIELD: 15 TO 20 SERVINGS

MIKE A. GIRARDI
STATION 93

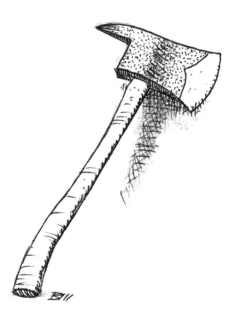

Chief Burton's Favorite District 69A: Beef Tips and Noodles

1 (3- TO 4-POUND) LONDON
    BROIL OR BEEF ROAST, CUT
    INTO ½-INCH-THICK STRIPS
SALT AND PEPPER TO TASTE
SEASONED SALT TO TASTE
3 TO 4 TABLESPOONS
    VEGETABLE OIL

2 ENVELOPES ONION SOUP MIX
3 ENVELOPES BROWN GRAVY MIX
2 CUPS SOUR CREAM
3 (12-OUNCE) PACKAGES EXTRA-
    WIDE EGG NOODLES

Sprinkle the beef with the salt, pepper and seasoned salt. Brown the beef in hot oil in a large pot. Add the soup mixes and stir to combine. Reduce the heat. Cook, covered, for 30 to 45 minutes or until the beef is tender, adding water if the mixture becomes dry.

Prepare the gravy using the package directions. Stir into the beef mixture. Add the sour cream and mix well. Simmer for 3 minutes longer.

Cook the noodles using the package directions. Drain and rinse. Place in a large serving bowl. Spoon the beef mixture over the noodles. Let stand for 5 to 10 minutes.

YIELD: 10 TO 12 SERVINGS

SCOTT S. GRANT
STATION 78

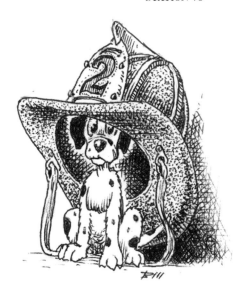

Captain Al's Sizzling Sirloin Tips

2 POUNDS BEEF SIRLOIN TIPS
1/4 TEASPOON FRESHLY GROUND
   PEPPER
1/2 TEASPOON UNSEASONED
   MEAT TENDERIZER
2 GARLIC CLOVES, FINELY
   MINCED
1/2 CUP FINELY CHOPPED ONION

1 1/4 CUPS LOW-SODIUM BEEF
   BROTH
1/3 CUP DRY RED WINE
1 TABLESPOON LIGHT SOY SAUCE
2 TABLESPOONS CORNSTARCH
1/4 CUP COLD WATER
1/4 CUP MINCED FRESH PARSLEY

Remove the fat from the sirloin tips. Cut into cubes and drain on paper towels. Sprinkle with the pepper and meat tenderizer. Brown on all sides in a nonstick skillet over medium-high heat, turning frequently. Add the garlic and onion. Cook until the onion is tender, stirring frequently. Stir in the broth, wine and soy sauce. Bring to a boil. Reduce the heat. Simmer, covered, for 1 1/2 hours or until the beef is tender.

Combine the cornstarch and cold water in a small bowl and stir until smooth. Pour into the beef mixture, stirring constantly. Cook until the mixture thickens, stirring constantly. Sprinkle the parsley over the top. Serve with hot cooked rice.

YIELD: 8 SERVINGS

LONNIE ALEXANDER
RETIRED

MEATS

No-Peek Beef

2 POUNDS BEEF, CUT INTO PIECES
1 ENVELOPE ONION SOUP MIX
1 CUP RED COOKING WINE
1 (10-OUNCE) CAN CREAM OF MUSHROOM SOUP
1 (4-OUNCE) JAR BUTTON MUSHROOMS, DRAINED
HOT COOKED RICE OR NOODLES

Combine the beef, soup mix, wine, soup and mushrooms in a large bowl and mix well. Spoon into a large baking dish. Bake, covered, at 300 degrees for 3 hours; do not peek.

Serve over hot cooked rice or noodles.

YIELD: 6 TO 8 SERVINGS

CHARLIE AND LINDA WILSON
FIRE ALARM

Fire Department Definitions

First In—The first arriving apparatus at a fire scene or emergency.

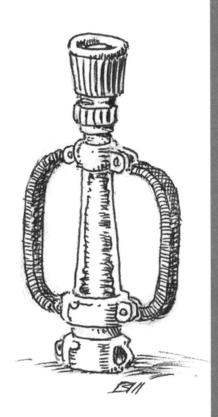

Beans Your Wife Can Cook

2 POUNDS GROUND BEEF
3 (16-OUNCE) CANS RANCH-STYLE BEANS
2 (16-OUNCE) CANS PORK AND BEANS

1 ONION, CHOPPED
1 BELL PEPPER, CHOPPED

Brown the ground beef in a skillet, stirring until crumbly; drain. Add the beans, onion and bell pepper and mix well. Bring to a simmer. Simmer for 1½ hours.

NOTE: After a long day of fighting fire in the Livable Forest (Kingwood), we tried a quick fix to end our hunger pains. The beans were quite tasty and filling. The thought entered our heads: "Hey, these are beans your wife could cook." So now the legend of these beans will live forever.

YIELD: 20 SERVINGS

DAVID W. CHILDERS
STATION 102

Hobo Supper Beans

2 POUNDS GROUND BEEF
1 ENVELOPE ONION SOUP MIX
1 (12-OUNCE) BOTTLE KETCHUP
1 CUP COLD WATER
¼ CUP MUSTARD

4 TEASPOONS VINEGAR
¼ CUP PACKED BROWN SUGAR
2 (30-OUNCE) CANS PORK AND BEANS

Brown the ground beef in a skillet, stirring until crumbly; drain. Add the soup mix, ketchup, cold water, mustard, vinegar, brown sugar and pork and beans and mix well. Spoon into a baking dish. Bake at 350 degrees for 1½ hours.

YIELD: 20 SERVINGS

HARVEY BIRDWELL
RETIRED

MEATS

Sam's Cabbage Rolls

2 LARGE HEADS GREEN CABBAGE
5 POUNDS GROUND ROUND
6 HAMBURGER BUNS, CRUMBLED
1 (10-OUNCE) CAN TOMATOES
   WITH GREEN CHILES
2 OR 3 RIBS CELERY, CHOPPED
2 BUNCHES GREEN ONIONS,
   CHOPPED
½ CUP RICE

4 EGGS
1 SMALL BELL PEPPER, CHOPPED
CHILI QUIK SEASONING TO TASTE
GRATED PARMESAN CHEESE
   TO TASTE
SALT AND PEPPER TO TASTE
4 (8-OUNCE) CANS TOMATO
   SAUCE

Cut the cabbage heads into halves. Bring enough water to cover the cabbage to a boil in a large saucepan. Add the cabbage. Cook until tender; drain. Separate the leaves.

Combine the ground round, crumbled hamburger buns, tomatoes, celery, green onions, rice, eggs, bell pepper, Chili Quik Seasoning, Parmesan cheese, salt and pepper in a large bowl and mix well.

Place 2 to 3 tablespoons of the ground round mixture on each cabbage leaf; use 2 leaves if they are small. Spread the mixture lengthwise along the leaves. Roll each leaf to enclose the filling. Arrange the stuffed leaves in 2 foil-lined pans. Pour 2 cans of tomato sauce over the leaves in each pan.

Bake, covered, at 450 degrees for 1 hour. You may also use the filling to stuff cooked bell pepper halves.

NOTE: Brian got this recipe years ago from a firefighter named Sam. This is a recipe that Brian and I made numerous times and it was always a hit.

YIELD: 15 TO 20 SERVINGS

ERMA MCLEROY
WIFE OF BRIAN MCLEROY, SR.

Beefy Enchiladas

2 POUNDS GROUND BEEF
2 ONIONS, CHOPPED
SALT AND PEPPER TO TASTE
1 (8-OUNCE) CAN TOMATO SAUCE
1 (6-OUNCE) CAN TOMATO PASTE
1 ENVELOPE ENCHILADA SAUCE
16 OUNCES HOT VELVEETA
   CHEESE

½ CUP VEGETABLE OIL
1 (36-COUNT) PACKAGE CORN
   TORTILLAS
3 CUPS SHREDDED CHEDDAR
   CHEESE

Brown the ground beef with ½ cup of the onions in a skillet, stirring until the ground beef is crumbly; drain. Season with salt and pepper. Stir in the tomato sauce and tomato paste.

Prepare the enchilada sauce using the package directions. Heat the Velveeta cheese in a saucepan until melted, adding a small amount of water to thin and stirring frequently.

Heat the oil in a skillet over medium-low heat. Dip each tortilla in the hot oil for 3 seconds on each side or until softened. Dip each tortilla in the enchilada sauce. Spread ¼ cup of the ground beef mixture down the center of each tortilla. Sprinkle the Cheddar cheese over the beef mixture. Roll to enclose the filling. Arrange over the bottom of a baking pan.

Pour the Velveeta cheese over the enchiladas. Pour any remaining enchilada sauce over the cheese. Bake at 350 degrees for 2 to 5 minutes. Sprinkle the remaining onion over the top. Bake for 10 minutes longer or until the cheese is bubbly.

YIELD: 18 SERVINGS

RAUL (GOOLEY) RIVERA
STATION 57

Enchi-Lasagna

1 POUND GROUND CHUCK

1/2 CUP CHOPPED ONION

SALT AND PEPPER TO TASTE

2 (8-OUNCE) CANS TOMATO
   SAUCE

3 TABLESPOONS CHILI POWDER

2 TEASPOONS CUMIN

1 (12-COUNT) PACKAGE CORN
   TORTILLAS

16 OUNCES (OR MORE) CHEDDAR
   CHEESE, SHREDDED

Brown the ground chuck with the onion, salt and pepper in a skillet, stirring until the ground chuck is crumbly; drain.

Heat the tomato sauce in a large saucepan over medium heat. Stir in the chili powder and cumin. Bring to a boil. Add the ground chuck mixture and mix well. Cut the tortillas into quarters.

Spread a small amount of the ground chuck mixture over the bottom of a baking dish. Alternate layers of tortillas, the remaining ground chuck mixture and Cheddar cheese in a baking dish until all ingredients are used. Sprinkle additional Cheddar cheese over the top. Bake at 350 degrees for 30 minutes or until bubbly.

YIELD: 4 TO 6 SERVINGS

AL YOUNG
STATION 69

Creole Lasagna

1 POUND ONIONS, CHOPPED

1 GARLIC CLOVE, MINCED

5 RIBS CELERY, CHOPPED

1 GREEN BELL PEPPER, CHOPPED

4 GREEN ONIONS, CHOPPED

CHOPPED PARSLEY TO TASTE

OLIVE OIL

16 OUNCES GROUND ROUND

16 OUNCES ITALIAN SAUSAGE

1 TEASPOON SALT

1/2 TEASPOON PEPPER

BASIL TO TASTE

OREGANO TO TASTE

1 (28-OUNCE) CAN ITALIAN
    TOMATOES

1 (15-OUNCE) CAN TOMATO
    SAUCE

2 (15-OUNCE) CANS TOMATO
    PASTE

30 OUNCES RICOTTA CHEESE

4 EGGS, BEATEN

1 CUP CHOPPED PARSLEY

1 TEASPOON SALT

1 TEASPOON PEPPER

2 1/2 CUPS GRATED ROMANO
    CHEESE

1/2 CUP GRATED PARMESAN
    CHEESE

16 OUNCES LASAGNA NOODLES,
    COOKED

2 POUNDS MOZZARELLA CHEESE,
    THINLY SLICED

Sauté the onions, garlic, celery, bell pepper, green onions and parsley to taste in olive oil in a skillet. Add the ground round and sausage. Cook until the ground round and sausage are brown and crumbly, stirring frequently; drain. Add 1 teaspoon salt, 1/2 teaspoon pepper, basil, oregano, tomatoes, tomato sauce and tomato paste and mix well. Bring to a simmer. Simmer for 3 to 4 hours, adding water as needed.

Combine the ricotta cheese, eggs, 1 cup parsley, 1 teaspoon salt, 1 teaspoon pepper, Romano cheese and Parmesan cheese in a bowl and mix well.

Layer the noodles, ricotta cheese mixture, mozzarella cheese slices and meat sauce 1/2 at a time in a large baking dish. Bake at 350 degrees for 1 hour.

YIELD: 20 SERVINGS

KAREN A. CAMBIAS
CAREER DEVELOPMENT

Mexican-Style Lasagna Casserole

2 POUNDS GROUND BEEF OR
 GROUND CHUCK
CHILI POWDER TO TASTE
2 TABLESPOONS TONY
 CHACHERE'S ORIGINAL
 SEASONING
1 BUNCH GREEN ONIONS,
 CHOPPED
1 (15-OUNCE) CAN WHOLE
 TOMATOES, CHOPPED

1 (16-OUNCE) CAN RANCH-STYLE
 BEANS
32 OUNCES VELVEETA CHEESE
1 (10-OUNCE) CAN TOMATOES
 WITH GREEN CHILES
1 LARGE PACKAGE CORN
 TORTILLAS

Brown the ground beef in a skillet, stirring until crumbly; drain. Add the chili powder and Tony Chachere's Original Seasoning and mix well. Add the green onions, tomatoes and beans and mix well. Bring to a simmer.

Cut the Velveeta cheese into chunks and place in a large saucepan. Heat until melted, stirring frequently. Add the tomatoes with green chiles and mix well.

Alternate layers of the ground beef mixture and cheese sauce in a 9×13-inch pan, arranging 6 tortillas between each layer and starting with the ground beef mixture and ending with the cheese sauce. Bake at 350 degrees for 30 minutes.

YIELD: 8 TO 10 SERVINGS

FRANK W. GRIZZAFFI
EMERGENCY OPERATIONS

Quick and Delicious Lasagna

5 POUNDS GROUND BEEF
2 BELL PEPPERS, CHOPPED
GARLIC TO TASTE
1 LARGE ONION, CHOPPED
SALT AND PEPPER TO TASTE
2 (16-OUNCE) PACKAGES
   LASAGNA NOODLES

3 (15-OUNCE) CANS HERB AND
   GARLIC TOMATO SAUCE
32 OUNCES VELVEETA CHEESE,
   SHREDDED

Brown the ground beef with the bell peppers, garlic and onion in a skillet, stirring until the ground beef is crumbly; drain. Season with salt and pepper. Cook the lasagna noodles using the package directions; drain.

Spread a thin layer of tomato sauce over the bottom of an 11×13-inch baking pan. Layer the noodles, remaining sauce and ground beef mixture alternately in the prepared pan until all of the ingredients are used. Sprinkle the Velveeta cheese over the top. Bake at 350 degrees until the cheese is bubbly.

NOTE: This goes well with the Yeast Bread on page 33.

YIELD: 15 TO 20 SERVINGS

MIKE A. GIRARDI
STATION 93

Spinach Lasagna

1 POUND GROUND BEEF OR
   GROUND TURKEY
1 (26-OUNCE) JAR SPAGHETTI
   SAUCE
1 CUP RICOTTA OR COTTAGE
   CHEESE
1/4 CUP GRATED PARMESAN
   CHEESE
1 EGG

1 (10-OUNCE) PACKAGE FROZEN
   CHOPPED SPINACH, THAWED
8 OUNCES LASAGNA NOODLES
16 OUNCES MOZZARELLA
   CHEESE, THINLY SLICED OR
   SHREDDED
GRATED PARMESAN CHEESE

Brown the ground beef in a skillet, stirring until crumbly; drain. Stir in the spaghetti sauce. Combine the ricotta cheese, 1/4 cup Parmesan cheese, egg and spinach in a bowl and mix well.

Set aside a small amount of the mozzarella cheese. Layer 1/2 of the ground beef mixture, 1/2 of the noodles, the ricotta cheese mixture, the mozzarella cheese, the remaining noodles and the remaining ground beef mixture in a 9×13-inch baking pan. Sprinkle the reserved mozzarella cheese and additional Parmesan cheese over the top. Cover with foil sprayed with nonstick baking spray.

Bake at 350 degrees for 1 hour. Let stand for 15 minutes.

YIELD: 10 TO 12 SERVINGS

KIMBERLY A. SMITH
STATION 13

Kimberly Smith

At the fire station, when it's your turn to cook, you prepare whatever you choose and the others can eat it or they can go without! When firefighter Kim Smith's turn came to cook, she chose Spinach Lasagna! You know, it wasn't that bad and I would gladly eat it every day if we could turn back time and have her back....

—Captain Larry Hunter,
Station 13

Kimberly, age 30, was a Houston firefighter for six years.

Lumpia

1 POUND GROUND PORK	2 EGGS
1 POUND GROUND BEEF	1 OR 2 PACKAGES LUMPIA
1 POUND CHOPPED SHRIMP	WRAPPERS
(OPTIONAL)	VEGETABLE OIL
4 LARGE CARROTS, FINELY	LUMPIA SAUCE
CHOPPED	
1 BUNCH GREEN ONIONS,	
CHOPPED	

Combine the pork, beef, shrimp, carrots, green onions and eggs in a large bowl and mix well. Spread about 1 heaping tablespoon of the mixture down the center of each wrapper. Roll to enclose the filling.

Heat oil in a skillet. Add the lumpia. Cook until golden brown on both sides. Serve over fried or steamed rice with Lumpia Sauce. You can find lumpia wrappers at oriental food markets.

YIELD: 8 TO 12 SERVINGS

RICK WATTERSON
STATION 51

Lumpia Sauce

1 CUP SUGAR	3 TABLESPOONS (HEAPING)
3 CUPS WATER	CORNSTARCH
3 TABLESPOONS SOY SAUCE	1½ TEASPOONS SALT

Heat the sugar in a saucepan over low heat until melted. Combine the water, soy sauce, cornstarch and salt in a small bowl and mix until smooth. Pour into the melted sugar. Cook until thickened, stirring constantly.

Meat Loaf

3 TO 4 POUNDS GROUND BEEF
1 MEDIUM ONION, CHOPPED
1 BELL PEPPER, CHOPPED
SALT AND PEPPER TO TASTE
2 EGGS

1 (6-OUNCE) PACKAGE (OR MORE)
    HERB-SEASONED STUFFING
    MIX
1 (8-OUNCE) CAN TOMATO SAUCE
KETCHUP

Combine the ground beef, onion, bell pepper, salt and pepper in a large bowl and mix well. Add the eggs and 2 cups of the stuffing mix and mix well. Add the tomato sauce and mix well. Add enough of the remaining stuffing mix to make a moist mixture.

Spoon into a 9×13-inch baking pan sprayed with nonstick cooking spray. Spread to the edges, leaving a mound in the middle.

Bake at 350 degrees for 1½ hours; drain. Spread a thick layer of ketchup over the top. Bake for an additional 10 to 15 minutes or until cooked through.

YIELD: 10 TO 15 SERVINGS

JEFF BOLES
STATION 37

Meat Loaf Italiano

3 (8-OUNCE) CANS PIZZA SAUCE
3 EGGS, BEATEN
3½ POUNDS GROUND BEEF
1 POUND ITALIAN SAUSAGE,
    CASING REMOVED

9 OUNCES VELVEETA, CHEESE
    SHREDDED
2¼ CUPS QUICK-COOKING OATS
1½ TEASPOONS ITALIAN
    SEASONING

Reserve ½ cup pizza sauce. Combine the remaining pizza sauce, eggs, ground beef, sausage, Velveeta cheese, oats and Italian seasoning in a bowl and mix well. Divide into 2 equal portions. Press each portion evenly into a loaf pan. Spread the reserved pizza sauce over the tops. Bake at 350 degrees for 1 hour or until cooked through.

YIELD: 10 SERVINGS

KEVIN S. THERAULT
STATION 6

PePe Mexican Pie

1 POUND GROUND ROUND
1 TABLESPOON CHILI POWDER
SALT TO TASTE
2 GARLIC CLOVES, CRUSHED
1 (4-OUNCE) CAN SLICED OLIVES
1/4 CUP CHOPPED ONION
1 CUP SOUR CREAM
2/3 CUP MAYONNAISE
CHOPPED JALAPEÑO CHILES OR
    HOT CHILES OF CHOICE TO
    TASTE

1 (8-COUNT) CAN CRESCENT
    ROLLS
2 MEDIUM TOMATOES, SLICED
1/4 CUP CHOPPED JALAPEÑO
    CHILES, GREEN CHILES
    OR A COMBINATION
    (OPTIONAL)
1 1/2 CUPS SHREDDED CHEDDAR
    CHEESE

Brown the ground round with the chili powder, salt and garlic in a skillet, stirring until the ground round is crumbly; drain. Combine the olives, onion, sour cream, mayonnaise and jalapeño chiles to taste in a separate bowl and mix well.

Unroll the crescent roll dough. Separate into triangles. Arrange over the bottom of a 10-inch pie plate with the triangles pointing inward. Press the edges to seal. Spoon the ground round mixture evenly over the dough. Arrange the tomato slices over the ground beef mixture. Sprinkle 1/4 cup jalapeño chiles and 1 cup of the Cheddar cheese over the ground beef mixture. Spread the sour cream mixture over the cheese. Sprinkle the remaining 1/2 cup Cheddar cheese over the top.

Bake at 375 degrees for 30 minutes or until the cheese is melted and the crust is golden brown. Let stand until slightly cooled.

NOTE: This is one of my biggest requests. I stole this one from my mother.

YIELD: 6 SERVINGS

DANIEL P. MATT
STATION 28

"Smilin' Eyes of Texas" Casserole

3 POUNDS LEAN GROUND BEEF
    OR TURKEY
3 (15-OUNCE) CANS BLACK-EYED
    PEAS
1 (10-OUNCE) CAN REDUCED-FAT
    CREAM OF CHICKEN SOUP
2 (10-OUNCE) CANS REDUCED-
    FAT CREAM OF MUSHROOM
    SOUP
1 (10-OUNCE) CAN HOT
    ENCHILADA SAUCE

1 LARGE ONION, CHOPPED
1 TEASPOON GARLIC POWDER
CHOPPED JALAPEÑO CHILES
    TO TASTE
1 (10-OUNCE) PACKAGE BAKED
    TORTILLA CHIPS
3 CUPS SHREDDED REDUCED-FAT
    COLBY JACK, CHEDDAR OR
    MOZZARELLA CHEESE

Brown the ground beef in a 4-quart kettle over medium heat, stirring until crumbly; drain. Add the black-eyed peas, cream of chicken soup, cream of mushroom soup, enchilada sauce, onion, garlic powder and chiles and mix well.

Spray two 8×10-inch baking dishes with nonstick cooking spray. Break the chips into pieces. Layer the chips, meat sauce and cheese ¼ at a time in each baking dish. Bake at 350 degrees for 35 minutes.

YIELD: 12 TO 16 SERVINGS

LARRY MCCLURE
STATION 31

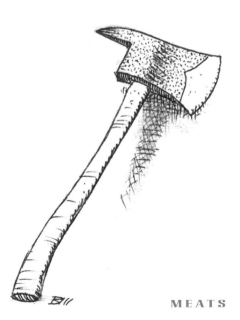

In July 1999, Station 93 celebrated its grand opening with a meal fit for firefighters! Delas Lancelin and Robert Marley, long-time firefighter chefs, created a full-course spread for the event. This day was especially important to them. After 15 years, they were working and cooking together again. "I taught Lancelin how to cook 18 years ago," says Marley. "And we used to cook up a storm!" (Together they have 41 combined years of service.)

Spaghetti Red

5 POUNDS GROUND BEEF	GARLIC TO TASTE
3 LARGE ONIONS, CHOPPED	CUMIN TO TASTE
3 BELL PEPPERS, CHOPPED	THYME TO TASTE
3 (10-OUNCE) CANS TOMATOES	OREGANO TO TASTE
WITH GREEN CHILES	6 TABLESPOONS CHILI POWDER
3 (14-OUNCE) CANS STEWED	16 OUNCES ELBOW MACARONI
TOMATOES	16 OUNCES SHELL MACARONI
1 (12-OUNCE) BOTTLE KETCHUP	16 OUNCES SPAGHETTI
SALT AND PEPPER TO TASTE	

Brown the ground beef with the onions and bell peppers in a large pot, stirring until the ground beef is crumbly; drain. Add the tomatoes, ketchup, salt, pepper, garlic, cumin, thyme, oregano and chili powder and mix well. Simmer for 45 minutes.

Cook the elbow macaroni, shell macaroni and spaghetti using the package directions; drain. Stir into the ground beef mixture. Serve immediately.

YIELD: 10 TO 12 SERVINGS

ROBERT MARLEY
STATION 93

Same Old Stuff (S.O.S.)

1 OR 2 YELLOW ONIONS
1 OR 2 BELL PEPPERS
5 POUNDS GROUND BEEF
3 OR 4 POTATOES
3 (10-OUNCE) CANS CREAM OF
   CHICKEN SOUP

2 (10-OUNCE) CANS CREAM OF
   MUSHROOM SOUP
1 QUART MILK
SALT AND PEPPER
1 OR 2 LOAVES OF SLICED BREAD

Chop the onions and bell peppers. Brown the ground beef with the onions and bell peppers in a large pot, stirring until the ground beef is crumbly; drain.

Peel the potatoes and cut into ¼-inch cubes. Combine the potatoes with enough water to cover in a saucepan. Bring to a boil. Boil until tender; drain.

Add the cream of chicken soup, cream of mushroom soup, milk and potatoes to the ground beef mixture and mix well. Bring to a simmer and cook until heated through. Season with salt and pepper.

Toast or brown the bread. Arrange the toast on individual plates. Spoon the ground beef mixture over the toast.

YIELD: 20 SERVINGS

RICKEY WOOD
FIRE ALARM

Station 31's "Stuff"

4 POUNDS GROUND CHUCK
1 (12-COUNT) PACKAGE CORN
    TORTILLAS, CUT INTO
    QUARTERS
2 LARGE YELLOW ONIONS,
    CHOPPED

4 (10-OUNCE) CANS CREAM OF
    CHICKEN SOUP
16 SLICES PROCESS CHEESE
2 (10-OUNCE) CANS TOMATOES
    WITH GREEN CHILES

Brown the ground chuck in a large skillet, stirring until crumbly; drain. Layer the ground chuck, corn tortillas, onions, soup, American cheese and tomatoes ½ at a time in an oblong baking dish. Bake at 350 degrees for 45 minutes.

YIELD: 8 TO 16 SERVINGS

MARSHALL SIMMONS
STATION 31

MEATS

Bailey's Stuffed Pasta Shells

4 POUNDS GROUND BEEF
1 ONION, CHOPPED
1 BELL PEPPER, CHOPPED
3 RIBS CELERY, CHOPPED
SALT AND PEPPER TO TASTE
GARLIC TO TASTE
ITALIAN SEASONING TO TASTE
½ TO 1 CUP WATER

30 LARGE PASTA SEASHELLS
3¾ CUPS RICOTTA CHEESE
1 BUNCH PARSLEY, FINELY
    CHOPPED
2 (15-OUNCE) CANS HERB AND
    GARLIC SPAGHETTI SAUCE

Brown the ground beef in a large skillet, stirring until crumbly; drain. Stir in the onion, bell pepper, celery, salt, pepper, garlic, Italian seasoning and enough water to make of the desired consistency. Bring to a simmer. Remove from the heat. Let stand until cool.

Cook the pasta using the package directions; drain. Let stand until cool.

Stuff each shell with 1 to 1½ tablespoons of the ground beef mixture. Top each with a small amount of ricotta cheese and sprinkle with parsley. Arrange in a baking dish. Pour enough spaghetti sauce around the shells to almost cover them. Bake, covered, at 350 degrees until bubbly.

YIELD: 15 TO 20 SERVINGS

HOBERT HOGGARD
STATION 16

Hogs Tamales

1½ POUNDS DRIED LARGE
   CORNHUSKS
1 (4-POUND) PORK SHOULDER
   ROAST
6 CUPS WATER
10 TO 12 TABLESPOONS CHILI
   POWDER
⅛ TEASPOON OREGANO

¼ TEASPOON CUMIN
2 TO 3 GARLIC CLOVES, MINCED
1 ONION, FINELY CHOPPED
SALT TO TASTE
2 CUPS SHORTENING
2 TABLESPOONS SALT
5 CUPS MASA HARINA

Remove the silks from the cornhusks and rinse. Soak in hot water for 10 minutes or until soft.

Combine the roast and 6 cups water in a large pot. Bring to a boil. Boil until tender. Drain, reserving the broth. Cut the roast into ¼-inch pieces.

Dissolve the chili powder in 1½ cups of the reserved broth in a large skillet. Add the pork. Stir in the oregano, cumin, garlic, onion and salt to taste. Cook until most of the liquid has evaporated.

Whip the shortening and 2 tablespoons salt in a mixing bowl until fluffy. Add the masa harina and 4⅓ cups of the reserved broth. Beat until light and fluffy or until a small amount floats in water.

Spread 2 tablespoons of the masa harina mixture in the center of 1 cornhusk. Place 1 tablespoon of the meat mixture over the masa harina mixture. Fold the sides of the cornhusk up to overlap in the center, bringing the pointed top down. Repeat with the remaining cornhusks. You may freeze the tamales at this point.

Stack the tamales in a steamer basket. Add 3 inches or more of water to a large saucepan. Bring to a boil. Place the steamer basket in the saucepan. Steam, covered, for 40 to 60 minutes or until cooked through.

NOTE: This recipe has become a family favorite around the holidays. This is an eight-hour process, but well worth the effort.

YIELD: 6 TO 8 TAMALES

ROBERT HOGGARD
STATION 35

Pittsburgh Pork Chops

14 CENTER LOIN PORK CHOPS
SALT AND PEPPER TO TASTE
TONY CHACHERE'S ORIGINAL
   SEASONING TO TASTE
GARLIC POWDER TO TASTE
2 (6-OUNCE) PACKAGES
   STUFFING MIX
2 ONIONS, CHOPPED

Season the pork chops with salt, pepper, Tony Chachere's Original Seasoning and garlic powder. Prepare the stuffing mix using the package directions.

Arrange 7 pork chops in a single layer over the bottom of a baking dish. Spoon the stuffing over the top and between each pork chop. Arrange the remaining 7 pork chops over the stuffing. Sprinkle the onions over the pork chops.

Bake, covered with foil, at 375 degrees for 1 hour. Serve with macaroni and Velveeta cheese, French-style green beans and applesauce.

NOTE: This is one of my favorites to cook at the fire station. Everyone loves it! (Firefighter Kevin Morrin has been cooking at fire stations for 16 years.)

YIELD: 7 SERVINGS

KEVIN P. MORRIN
STATION 76

Fire Station 76

Station 76 is tucked away in far southwest Houston, just inside the city limits, near Alief. Known proudly as the "Spirit of 76," the station opened in 1985. The crews experienced a tragic loss on February 14, 2000. Firefighters Lewis Mayo and Kimberly Smith lost their lives while battling an early-morning fire at a McDonald's restaurant. Today, a permanent granite monument is cemented in the front lawn of the station in memory of Lewis and Kim.

Stuffed Pork Chops

2 (6-OUNCE) PACKAGES STUFFING MIX
12 BONELESS CENTER CUT PORK CHOPS
SALT AND PEPPER TO TASTE
GARLIC POWDER TO TASTE
MRS. DASH SEASONING TO TASTE

Prepare the stuffing mix using the package directions.

Butterfly the pork chops. Spoon the stuffing into the pork chops. Sprinkle the pork chops with salt, pepper, garlic powder and Mrs. Dash seasoning. Arrange in a single layer in a foil-lined baking pan.

Bake at 350 degrees for 45 minutes or until cooked through.

YIELD: 6 SERVINGS

ROBERT MARLEY
STATION 93

Pork Chops with Wild Rice Dressing

VEGETABLE OIL

1 LARGE ONION, CHOPPED

GARLIC SALT TO TASTE

SALT AND PEPPER TO TASTE

SAGE TO TASTE

2 (10-OUNCE) CANS CHICKEN
    BROTH

3 (10-OUNCE) PACKAGES WILD
    RICE

12 TO 14 PORK CHOPS

1 (8-INCH) SKILLET OF CORN
    BREAD, CRUMBLED

Heat a small amount of vegetable oil in a roasting pan. Sauté the onion in the hot oil. Stir in the garlic salt, salt, pepper and sage. Add enough water to come halfway up the sides of the pan. Pour in the broth. Stir in the rice. Arrange the pork chops over the top. Bake at 375 degrees for 45 minutes. Stir in the corn bread. Bake until thickened and top is brown. Serve with cranberry sauce.

YIELD: 6 OR 7 SERVINGS

JAY S. EVANS
PUBLIC INFORMATION

The Chief and the Steak

The chief at the firehouse was working feverishly in an attempt to prepare a plate-size T-bone steak for broiling. He placed it into the oven and the speaker cracked open. He quickly moved it from the oven to the icebox for safekeeping (so he thought). Four hours later, the chief returned. That alarm had gone to a three-alarm fire. His mouth salivating, he jerked the icebox door open. No steak! No plate! No fork! Scowling he looked at the oven (surely not). He jerked the oven open. With a look of exasperation, his blue piercing eyes turned red and out of his mouth came a barrage of profanity befitting only a soldier who had been in battle...only to be defeated. There was his plate with the remaining meatless T-bone center, fork at its side and a note on top with the words: Thank you very much.

This culinary case remains open in the annals of the history of the Houston Fire Department. And no one has been brave enough to come forward.

"Afterburner" Casserole

2 POUNDS HOT OR REGULAR
   BULK TURKEY SAUSAGE
1 CUP CHOPPED ONION
2 CUPS CHOPPED CELERY
3 OUNCES SLICED JALAPEÑO
   CHILES OR 3 OUNCES MILD
   PICANTE SAUCE
1 (8-OUNCE) CAN SLICED WATER
   CHESTNUTS, DRAINED

1 (4-OUNCE) CAN SLICED
   MUSHROOMS, DRAINED
1 (10-OUNCE) CAN CHICKEN
   NOODLE SOUP
1 CUP WATER
1 CUP RICE
½ TEASPOON SALT
½ TEASPOON PEPPER
1 CUP BOILING WATER

Brown the sausage in a 4-quart kettle, stirring until crumbly. Drain the sausage, reserving 3 tablespoons of the drippings. Set the sausage aside.

Sauté the onion and celery in the reserved drippings in the kettle. Stir in the sausage, jalapeño chiles, water chestnuts, mushrooms, soup, water, rice, salt, pepper and boiling water. Spoon into a 3-quart baking dish sprayed with nonstick cooking spray.

Bake, covered with foil, at 350 degrees for 1 hour, stirring after 30 minutes.

YIELD: 10 TO 12 SERVINGS

LARRY MCCLURE
STATION 31

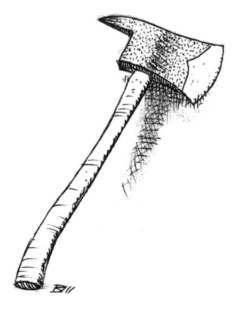

MEATS

Ravioli

16 OUNCES HOT SAUSAGE
16 OUNCES BOW TIE PASTA
1 (10-OUNCE) PACKAGE CHOPPED
   SPINACH
1 ONION, CHOPPED

1 EGG, BEATEN
1 CUP PLAIN BREAD CRUMBS
1 (10-OUNCE) CAN TOMATO SOUP
16 OUNCES SHREDDED CHEDDAR
   CHEESE

Brown the sausage in a skillet, stirring until crumbly; drain. Cook the pasta using the package directions; drain. Cook the spinach using the package directions. Drain, pressing out the excess moisture.

Combine the sausage, spinach, onion, egg and bread crumbs in a bowl and mix well. Grease the bottom of a 1½-quart baking dish. Layer the pasta, sausage mixture, soup and cheese ½ at a time in the baking dish.

Bake at 350 degrees for 30 minutes or until heated through.

YIELD: 4 TO 6 SERVINGS

KENNETH BOLES
STATION 103

Pasta Delight

16 OUNCES PASTA SHELLS OR
   ROTINI
1 ENVELOPE ALFREDO PASTA
   PRIMA MIX
1 (8-OUNCE) BOTTLE LIGHT
   ITALIAN SALAD DRESSING

12 OUNCES SHREDDED PIZZA
   CHEESE
2 RIBS CELERY, CHOPPED
16 OUNCES PEPPERONI,
   CHOPPED

Cook the pasta using the package directions; drain. Combine the Alfredo Pasta Prima mix and salad dressing in a large bowl and mix well.

Add the cheese, celery, pepperoni and pasta to the dressing mixture and mix well. Chill, covered, until ready to serve.

YIELD: 4 SERVINGS

ROBERT G. PARRY
EMS

As a rookie I had an experience involving dinner once at Station 16. We had spaghetti for dinner and it was great, so I went back for seconds. Somewhere between my first huge plate and the second, my 32-ounce glass of water kicked in. I found myself unable to eat another bite. As I made my way toward the trash can I was stopped and was told there was a rule, "Eat it or Wear it." Returning to the table, now with a crowd of onlookers, I slowly, over the next 30 minutes, cleaned my plate. I was miserable. All I could do was pray that we didn't get a run.

—Kenneth Boles

Rigatoni Casserole

6 LINKS HOT ITALIAN SAUSAGE, CASINGS REMOVED	2 (15-OUNCE) CANS ITALIAN TOMATO SAUCE
1/4 CUP ITALIAN SEASONING	2 (16-OUNCE) PACKAGES RIGATONI PASTA
2 (15-OUNCE) CANS CHOPPED TOMATOES	24 OUNCES MOZZARELLA CHEESE, SHREDDED
2 (10-OUNCE) CANS TOMATOES WITH GREEN CHILES	

Brown the sausage in a skillet, stirring until crumbly; drain. Stir in the Italian seasoning. Add the tomatoes and tomato sauce and mix well. Bring to a simmer.

Cook the rigatoni using the package directions; drain. Stir into the sausage mixture. Spoon the sausage mixture into a baking pan. Sprinkle the cheese over the top. Bake at 350 degrees for 20 to 30 minutes.

YIELD: 10 SERVINGS

KEVIN S. THERAULT
STATION 6

Dill Sauce

1 CUP MAYONNAISE	2 TABLESPOONS PARSLEY
1 CUP SOUR CREAM	SALT TO TASTE
1 TABLESPOON DILL	LAWRY'S SEASONING TO TASTE

Combine the mayonnaise, sour cream, dill, parsley, salt and Lawry's seasoning in a bowl and mix well. Chill, covered, until ready to serve. Serve with chicken or steak.

YIELD: 16 (2-TABLESPOON) SERVINGS

LISA HAVLICE
STATION 18

Haz Mat Habanero Hot Sauce

1 (30-OUNCE) CAN PEACH
    HALVES, DRAINED
1 (20-OUNCE) JAR PEACH
    PRESERVES

1 HABANERO CHILE
2 JALAPEÑO CHILES
2 SERRANO CHILES
JUICE OF 1 LIME

Process the peach halves in a blender until almost smooth. Add the preserves and pulse once. Seed and chop the habanero chile, jalapeño chiles and serrano chiles. Add the chopped chiles and lime juice to the peach mixture. Process until of the desired consistency, adding additional chiles if desired.

YIELD: 50 (2-TABLESPOON) SERVINGS

TOMMY ERICKSON
STATION 22

Pure Creole Seasoning

1 CUP SALT
½ CUP GARLIC POWDER
½ CUP ONION POWDER
3 TABLESPOONS PAPRIKA
3 TABLESPOONS CRUSHED
    BASIL LEAVES
3 TABLESPOONS THYME

2 TABLESPOONS CAYENNE
    PEPPER
1 TABLESPOON RED PEPPER
    (OPTIONAL)
2 TABLESPOONS WHITE PEPPER
½ CUP MINUS 1 TEASPOON DRY
    MUSTARD

Combine the salt, garlic powder, onion powder, paprika, basil, thyme, cayenne pepper, red pepper, white pepper and dry mustard in a bowl and mix well. Serve on steak, grits, fish, chicken, potatoes, salad or vegetables.

YIELD: 3¼ CUPS

KAREN A. CAMBIAS
CAREER DEVELOPMENT

WELL, SO MUCH FOR KING RANCH CHICKEN!
IT LOOKS LIKE EMORY'S SPECIAL AGAIN TONIGHT:
HOT DOGS A LA CARTE!

A Fire Every Time

When I was the cook at Station 25 on the old B shift, this was a requested meal because every time it was cooked, we were guaranteed a fire that night. Cooking might begin at 2 or 3 in the afternoon but dinner might not be served until midnight because those blooming fires interrupted our cooking or meal. This is a delicious meal. Enjoy! (This recipe backfired one night. At Station 35 I cooked this meal to break a slow streak. We made no fires that night, but Engine 25 made two that night according to Captain Clifford Reed. Captain Reed says thanks.)

Chicken à la Wendy

1 (3-POUND) CHICKEN
3 (10-OUNCE) PACKAGES
   CHOPPED BROCCOLI
3 (10-OUNCE) CANS CREAM OF
   CHICKEN SOUP
2 CUPS MAYONNAISE

1 TABLESPOON LEMON JUICE
SALT AND PEPPER TO TASTE
1 CUP SHREDDED CHEDDAR
   CHEESE
¼ CUP BREAD CRUMBS
   (OPTIONAL)

Combine the chicken with enough water to cover in a large pot. Bring to a simmer. Simmer until the chicken is tender and cooked through; drain. Chop the chicken, discarding the skin and bones. Cook the broccoli using the package directions; drain. Combine the soup, mayonnaise and lemon juice in a bowl and mix well.

Arrange the broccoli over the bottom of a 9×13-inch baking dish. Arrange the chicken over the broccoli. Spread the mayonnaise mixture over the chicken. Sprinkle with salt and pepper. Sprinkle the cheese over the mayonnaise mixture. Sprinkle the bread crumbs over the top. Bake at 350 degrees for 20 minutes or until bubbly and the cheese is melted.

YIELD: 10 TO 12 SERVINGS

ROBERT HOGGARD
STATION 35

Chicken and Dumplings

1 LARGE CHICKEN
1 LARGE ONION, CHOPPED
6 RIBS CELERY, CHOPPED
6 CARROTS, CHOPPED
1 (16-OUNCE) CAN CREAM OF
   CHICKEN SOUP

SALT AND PEPPER TO TASTE
2/3 CUP MILK
2 CUPS BAKING MIX
1 (16-OUNCE) CAN SWEET PEAS,
   DRAINED

Combine the chicken with enough water to cover in a stockpot. Bring to a boil. Add the onion and celery. Boil until the chicken is tender and cooked through. Remove the chicken. Reduce the heat. Simmer the broth. Let the chicken stand until cooled. Chop the chicken, discarding the skin and bones. Add to the broth. Add the carrots, soup, salt and pepper to the chicken mixture and mix well. Simmer the chicken mixture.

Combine the milk and baking mix in a bowl and mix well. Roll 1/2 inch thick on a lightly floured surface. Cut into 1-inch squares. Place in the chicken mixture. Cook for 10 minutes. Stir in the peas. Cook, covered, for 10 minutes.

NOTE: This recipe feeds three firefighters per chicken or a family of four. I double the recipe for every three firefighters and alternate with chicken mushroom soup or cream of celery soup.

YIELD: 3 OR 4 SERVINGS

CAPTAIN MERRILL WOOD
STATION 16

Chicken Jacuzzi

2 CHICKENS, OR 5 TO 6 POUNDS CHICKEN LEG QUARTERS
SEASONED SALT OR TONY CHACHERE'S ORIGINAL SEASONING
VEGETABLE OIL
1 ONION, CHOPPED

2 (10-OUNCE) CANS CREAM OF CHICKEN SOUP
2 (10-OUNCE) CANS CREAM OF CELERY SOUP
1 (15-OUNCE) CAN MEXICAN-STYLE STEWED TOMATOES, DRAINED
HOT COOKED RICE

Cut the chickens into pieces. Sprinkle with the seasoned salt. Heat oil in a large ovenproof pot. Add the onion. Add the chicken. Cook until the onion is tender and chicken changes color, stirring constantly. Remove from the heat.

Combine the chicken soup and celery soup in a bowl and mix well. Add the tomatoes and mix well. Pour over the chicken. Stir to evenly coat the chicken pieces.

Bake, covered, at 350 degrees for 2 hours, stirring every 30 minutes. Serve over hot cooked rice.

YIELD: 6 TO 8 SERVINGS

JEFF BOLES
STATION 37

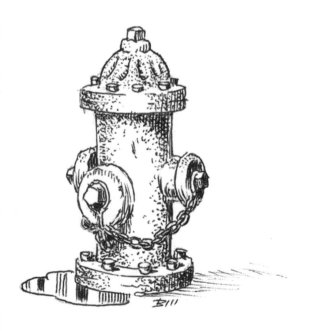

Chicken Mole Enchiladas

1 (8-OUNCE) JAR MOLE

1 CUP (ABOUT) CHICKEN STOCK

1 CUP SOUR CREAM

1 CHICKEN, COOKED, BONED,
    SKIN REMOVED, SHREDDED

2 TABLESPOONS (OR MORE) CORN
    OIL

48 CORN TORTILLAS

12 OUNCES MONTEREY JACK
    CHEESE, SHREDDED

4 GREEN ONIONS, CHOPPED

CHIVES

Cook the mole in a skillet over low heat, stirring frequently. Stir in the stock. Cook until smooth, stirring frequently. Set aside.

Combine the sour cream and chicken in a bowl and mix well. Heat the oil in a skillet until hot. Dip a tortilla in the oil until soft. Drain on paper towels. Dip in the mole sauce, coating both sides. Spread 1 tablespoon of the chicken mixture down the center of the tortilla. Roll to enclose the filling. Place in a baking dish. Repeat with the remaining tortillas.

Spoon any remaining mole sauce over the enchiladas. Sprinkle the cheese over the top. Broil under a preheated broiler until the cheese melts. Garnish with the green onions and chives.

NOTE: We like this dish because it's rich and fattening! Unfortunately, firefighters don't have any trouble eating this kind of food!

YIELD: 24 SERVINGS   STATION 27

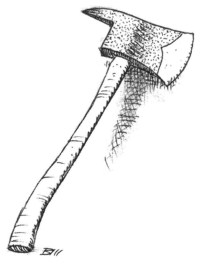

Spicy Chicken and Rice

2 CHICKENS
1 ONION, CHOPPED
2 CUPS CHOPPED CELERY
2 (10-OUNCE) CANS TOMATOES WITH GREEN CHILES
2 GARLIC CLOVES, CHOPPED
¼ CUP CHOPPED PARSLEY (OPTIONAL)
2½ CUPS RICE
SALT AND PEPPER TO TASTE

Combine the chickens, onion, celery, tomatoes, garlic and parsley in a large pot. Add enough water to cover. Bring to a boil. Boil until the chickens are tender and cooked through. Remove the chickens. Add the rice to the hot broth. Reduce the heat and simmer.

Chop the chicken, discarding the skin and bones. Stir into the rice mixture. Cook until the rice is tender. Season with salt and pepper.

YIELD: 6 SERVINGS

DONNIE HAVEMANN
STATION 15

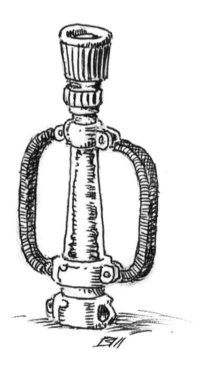

Chicken Spaghetti

5 CHICKENS
2 BELL PEPPERS
2 LARGE ONIONS
1 (15-OUNCE) CAN PEELED
    WHOLE TOMATOES
VEGETABLE OIL
8 OUNCES MUSHROOMS,
    SLICED

5 (6-OUNCE) CANS TOMATO
    SAUCE
2 (6-OUNCE) CANS TOMATO
    PASTE
3 POUNDS VELVEETA CHEESE,
    CHOPPED
1 (48-OUNCE) PACKAGE
    SPAGHETTI

Combine the chickens with enough water to cover in a large pot. Bring to a boil. Boil until the chickens are tender and cooked through.

Remove the chickens, discarding the broth. Chop the chicken, discarding the skin and bones.

Chop the bell peppers, onions and tomatoes. Sauté the bell peppers and onions in a small amount of oil in a large saucepan. Add the mushrooms, tomatoes, tomato sauce and tomato paste. Bring to a simmer.

Add the Velveeta cheese to the tomato mixture gradually, stirring constantly. Stir in the chicken and simmer.

Cook the spaghetti using the package directions. Drain and place in a large bowl. Spoon the chicken mixture over the spaghetti.

YIELD: 30 SERVINGS

GENE M. KENDALL, SR.
EMERGENCY OPERATIONS

Cheesy Chicken Spaghetti

2 CHICKENS, OR 4 TO 5 POUNDS
  CHICKEN BREASTS
SALT AND PEPPER TO TASTE
16 OUNCES VELVEETA CHEESE,
  SHREDDED
4 RIBS CELERY, CHOPPED
1 GREEN BELL PEPPER, CHOPPED
1 MEDIUM ONION, CHOPPED
2 GARLIC CLOVES, CRUSHED

1 (4-OUNCE) CAN MUSHROOM
  PIECES
1 (16-OUNCE) PACKAGE
  SPAGHETTI, BROKEN
1 (16-OUNCE) CAN TOMATOES
  WITH GREEN CHILES
1 (10-OUNCE) CAN CREAM OF
  MUSHROOM SOUP
PAPRIKA TO TASTE

Combine the chickens with enough water to cover in a large pot. Season with salt and pepper. Bring to a simmer. Simmer until the chickens are tender and cooked through. Remove the chickens and reserve 4 cups of the chicken broth. Chop the chicken, discarding the skin and bones. Combine the chicken and Velveeta cheese in a bowl and toss together.

Combine the reserved broth, celery, bell pepper, onion, garlic and mushrooms in a large pot. Cook for 2 minutes. Add the spaghetti. Cook until tender. Stir in the tomatoes and soup. Season with salt, pepper and paprika. Stir in the chicken mixture.

YIELD: 10 TO 12 SERVINGS

ANDY COE
STATION 16

POULTRY

Station 21's Chicken Surprise

4 CHICKENS
SEASONED SALT
PEPPER
GARLIC POWDER
4 (32-OUNCE) CANS MIXED VEGETABLES
3 (26-OUNCE) CANS CREAM OF CHICKEN SOUP

Cut the chickens into pieces. Sprinkle with the seasoned salt, pepper and garlic powder. Arrange in a large roasting pan. Bake at 450 degrees for 1 hour; drain.

Combine the vegetables and soup in a bowl and mix well. Spoon over and between the chicken pieces. Bake for 45 minutes. Serve over hot cooked white rice.

NOTE: This is the only thing that I got from my wife in the divorce.

YIELD: 10 SERVINGS

JAMES ELI
STATION 21

Station 21 is located less than a mile west of the Houston Astrodome. A district station, Station 21 houses an ambulance, engine, ladder truck, and a district chief. It was built in 1972.

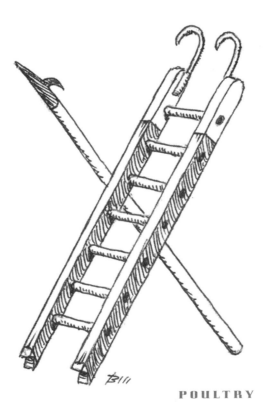

POULTRY

McLeroy's King Ranch Casserole

1 CHICKEN
1 (10-OUNCE) CAN CREAM OF
    CHICKEN SOUP
1 (10-OUNCE) CAN CREAM OF
    CELERY SOUP
1 (10-OUNCE) CAN TOMATOES
    WITH GREEN CHILES

½ TO 1 ONION, CHOPPED
1 (9-OUNCE) PACKAGE NACHO
    CHEESE TORTILLA CHIPS
1 TO 2 CUPS SHREDDED
    CHEDDAR CHEESE

Trim the chicken. Combine the chicken with enough water to cover in a large pot. Bring to a boil. Boil until the chicken is tender and cooked through. Remove the chicken and reserve 1½ cups of the chicken broth. Chop the chicken, discarding the skin and bones.

Combine the chicken, reserved broth, cream of chicken soup, cream of celery soup, tomatoes and onion in a bowl and mix well.

Sprinkle the chips over the bottom of a 9×13-inch baking dish. Spoon the chicken mixture evenly over the chips. Sprinkle the cheese over the top. Bake at 350 degrees for 30 minutes.

You may substitute one 10-count package of flour tortillas torn into small pieces for the tortilla chips.

NOTE: This is a favorite at the fire station. I got it a long time ago and turned it on to the fire station.

YIELD: 6 TO 8 SERVINGS

BRIAN MCLEROY
STATION 45

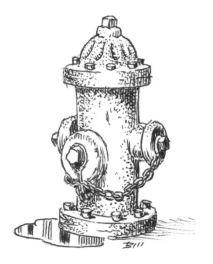

Chicken Parmesan

¼ TO ½ CUP CHOPPED ONION

1 OR 2 GARLIC CLOVES, MINCED

OLIVE OIL

1 (10-OUNCE) CAN TOMATO
    PURÉE

1 (8-OUNCE) CAN TOMATO SAUCE

2 TEASPOONS ITALIAN
    SEASONING

¼ TEASPOON SALT

2 EGGS, BEATEN

2 TABLESPOONS MILK OR WATER

4 BONELESS SKINLESS CHICKEN
    BREAST HALVES

ITALIAN SEASONED BREAD
    CRUMBS

16 OUNCES MOZZARELLA
    CHEESE, SLICED ¼ INCH
    THICK

GRATED PARMESAN CHEESE

Sauté the onion and garlic in a small amount of olive oil in a skillet; drain. Add the tomato purée, tomato sauce, Italian seasoning and salt and mix well. Reduce the heat to low. Cook until heated through.

Combine the eggs and milk in a shallow dish and mix well. Dip the chicken in the egg mixture and coat with bread crumbs. Brown the chicken on both sides in olive oil in a skillet over medium-high heat. Coat the bottom of a 9×13-inch baking pan with olive oil or nonstick cooking spray. Arrange the chicken in the prepared pan. Place the slices of mozzarella cheese over the chicken. Spoon the tomato mixture over the cheese slices. Sprinkle with the Parmesan cheese. Bake at 350 degrees for 1 hour.

YIELD: 4 SERVINGS

ROGER WESTHOFF
STATION 68

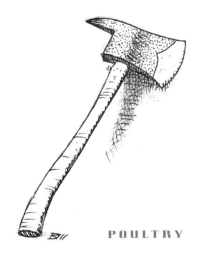

POULTRY

123

Chicken and Rice

8 OUNCES MUSHROOMS, SLICED

1 ONION, CHOPPED

1 TABLESPOON BUTTER

4 POUNDS BONELESS SKINLESS
　　CHICKEN BREASTS

¾ CUP ITALIAN SALAD DRESSING

½ TEASPOON SALT

PEPPER TO TASTE

SEASONED SALT TO TASTE

6 (14-OUNCE) CANS CHICKEN
　　BROTH

3 CUPS RICE

Sauté the mushrooms and onion in the butter in a large skillet. Cut the chicken into bite-size pieces. Add the chicken pieces, salad dressing, salt, pepper and seasoned salt to the mushroom mixture. Cook, covered, for 3 to 5 minutes or until the chicken is white. Remove the chicken and keep warm.

Add the broth and rice to the mushrooms and onion and mix well. Cook, covered, for 18 to 20 minutes or until the rice is tender. Stir in the chicken. Let stand for 5 minutes. You may adjust the amount of rice, using 2 cans of broth for every cup of rice.

YIELD: 8 TO 10 SERVINGS

STEVE LEVELL
STATION 75

East End Grilled
Spicy Chicken Breast Fillets

8 (4-OUNCE) BONELESS SKINLESS
    CHICKEN BREASTS
1 SMALL GARLIC CLOVE,
    CRUSHED
1 SMALL ONION, FINELY
    CHOPPED
1 TO 2 TABLESPOONS FINELY
    CHOPPED CILANTRO

2 TO 3 TABLESPOONS FRESH
    LIME JUICE
2 TABLESPOONS OLIVE OIL
1/2 TEASPOON CHILI POWDER
FRESHLY GROUND PEPPER
    TO TASTE

Arrange the chicken in a single layer in a shallow glass dish. Combine the garlic, onion, cilantro, lime juice, olive oil, chili powder and pepper in a bowl and mix well. Pour over the chicken. Refrigerate, covered, for 2 to 3 hours, turning the chicken occasionally; drain.

Place on a grill over hot coals or wood. Grill for 6 to 7 minutes or until cooked through, turning once. You may broil the chicken instead of grilling.

NOTE: A hint from retired senior captain and fire station Chef Extraordinaire Dennis Pena, "If cooking on an outdoor grill and you are using wood to grill, stay away from Chinese Tallow. I know."

YIELD: 8 SERVINGS

STATION 20 SMOKE DIVERS

To gear up for a day's work at their east end fire station, Station 20 is not complete without homemade hot sauce every day. The captain and chief on duty give it their seal of approval before everyone dives in with the chips. Captain Rivera uses the sweat on his bald spot to gauge the temperature. "When my bald spot starts sweating, I know it's good!" The industrial-size bowl lasts throughout the day to accompany most every meal and snack.

Built in 1973, Station 20 sits at the intersection of Navigation Street and Macario Garcia. Its response area includes Houston's Ship Channel, refineries, warehouses, and near downtown businesses. They also protect the Magnolia and Central Park subdivisions.

Fire Station Chicken Cordon Bleu

BONELESS SKINLESS CHICKEN
BREAST HALVES
ITALIAN BREAD CRUMBS

CHOPPED HAM
SWISS CHEESE SLICES

Dredge the chicken in the bread crumbs to coat. Arrange in a baking dish. Sprinkle the ham over the chicken. Place a slice of Swiss cheese over each chicken breast. Bake at 350 degrees for 30 minutes or until cooked through.

YIELD: VARIABLE

KEVIN S. THERAULT
STATION 6

Extra Tap Tetrazzini

1 MEDIUM ONION, CHOPPED
1/2 CUP CHOPPED CELERY
2 TABLESPOONS MARGARINE
16 OUNCES VELVEETA CHEESE,
CUBED
1 (10-OUNCE) CAN CREAM OF
CHICKEN SOUP

1 PACKAGE MEDIUM EGG
NOODLES
CHICKEN BROTH
1 CHICKEN, COOKED, BONED

Cook the onion and celery in the margarine in a large skillet until the onion is brown, stirring frequently. Add the Velveeta cheese and soup. Cook over low heat until the cheese is melted, stirring constantly.

Cook the noodles using the package directions, substituting chicken broth for the water. Drain, reserving 3/4 cup of the broth. Stir the reserved broth into the cheese mixture. Add the chicken and noodles and mix well. Cook for 2 minutes or until heated through.

YIELD: 4 TO 6 SERVINGS

GARY PICK
STATION 7

"Totally Involved" Chicken Casserole

6 (4-OUNCE) BONELESS SKINLESS
    CHICKEN BREAST HALVES
½ TEASPOON CUMIN
1 (10-OUNCE) CAN REDUCED-FAT
    CREAM OF MUSHROOM SOUP
1 (10-OUNCE) CAN TOMATOES
    WITH GREEN CHILES,
    DRAINED
4 OUNCES NONFAT PROCESS
    CHEESE LOAF, CUBED

1 CUP COOKED LONG GRAIN RICE
¾ CUP NONFAT SOUR CREAM
1 CUP CRUSHED BAKED
    TORTILLA CHIPS
½ CUP SHREDDED FAT-FREE
    CHEDDAR CHEESE
½ TEASPOON CHILI POWDER

Cut the chicken into 1-inch pieces. Sprinkle with the cumin. Heat a large nonstick skillet coated with nonstick cooking spray over medium-high heat until hot. Add the chicken. Cook for 5 minutes or until browned, stirring constantly. Reduce the heat to medium.

Add the soup, tomatoes and process cheese. Cook until the cheese melts, stirring occasionally. Remove from the heat. Add the rice and sour cream and mix well. Spoon into a 9×13-inch baking dish. Sprinkle the tortilla chips over the chicken mixture.

Bake at 375 degrees for 20 minutes. Sprinkle the Cheddar cheese and chili powder over the top. Bake for an additional 5 minutes or until the cheese melts.

YIELD: 10 TO 12 SERVINGS

LARRY MCCLURE
STATION 31

POULTRY

Fire Department Definitions

Didn't Turn a Wheel—Did not make any calls during a shift or referenced time period. A rare treat!

Make Fire Chicken

½ CUP (1 STICK) BUTTER
5 POUNDS BONELESS SKINLESS
    CHICKEN BREAST HALVES
6 CUPS HEAVY CREAM
1 CUP WHITE COOKING WINE

1 CUP COLD WATER
CORNSTARCH
2 (21-OUNCE) PACKAGES BOIL-IN-
    A-BAG RICE
SALT AND PEPPER TO TASTE

Heat the butter in a large skillet until melted. Add the chicken. Cook until browned on both sides. Remove from the skillet and set aside. Reduce the heat to medium.

Pour the cream into the skillet. Stir in the wine. Combine the cold water with enough cornstarch to thicken the cream mixture in a small bowl and stir until smooth. Stir into the cream mixture. Cook until the mixture begins to thicken, stirring constantly. Add the chicken to the cream mixture. Reduce the heat to low. Cook until the chicken is tender.

Cook the rice using the package directions. Serve the chicken and gravy over the rice. Season with salt and pepper.

NOTE: This recipe has a history of causing things to start hopping around the fire station. It seems to even stir up things in the streets. We've made numerous house fires the evenings we cooked this meal, so only serve it when you feel the challenge is able to be met.

YIELD: 8 SERVINGS

RANDALL CURRIE
STATION 34

POULTRY

Nancy's Stuffed Chicken Breasts

2 (6-OUNCE) PACKAGES CORN BREAD STUFFING MIX
8 CHICKEN BREASTS
SALT AND PEPPER TO TASTE
GARLIC POWDER TO TASTE
PAPRIKA TO TASTE
8 SLICES MOZZARELLA CHEESE

Prepare the stuffing using the package directions.

Cut a slit in the thickest portion of each chicken breast, creating a pocket. Place 1/4 cup of the stuffing in each pocket. Sprinkle the salt, pepper, garlic powder and paprika over the chicken. Place in a baking pan.

Bake at 350 degrees for 1 to 1 1/2 hours or until cooked through. Place a slice of cheese over each chicken breast. Let stand until cheese is melted. Serve immediately.

YIELD: 8 SERVINGS

HOBERT HOGGARD
STATION 16

Chicken Potpie

1 (4-POUND) CHICKEN
1 TABLESPOON ITALIAN
    SEASONING
1 TEASPOON MINCED GARLIC
1 TABLESPOON SALT
1 (16-OUNCE) PACKAGE FROZEN
    MIXED VEGETABLES
1 POTATO, PEELED, CUBED
1 (10-OUNCE) CAN CREAM OF
    MUSHROOM SOUP

1½ CUPS YELLOW CORNMEAL
½ CUP FLOUR
4 TEASPOONS BAKING POWDER
½ TEASPOON SALT
⅓ CUP SUGAR
1 CUP MILK
2 EGGS
¼ CUP VEGETABLE OIL

Combine the chicken, Italian seasoning, garlic and 1 tablespoon salt in a large stockpot. Add just enough water to cover the chicken. Bring to a boil. Boil until the chicken is tender and cooked through. Remove the chicken, reserving the broth. Chop the chicken, discarding the skin and bones.

Boil the broth until reduced by half. Add the mixed vegetables and potato. Reduce the heat to low. Simmer for 10 minutes. Remove from the heat. Stir in the soup and chicken.

Combine the cornmeal, flour, baking powder, ½ teaspoon salt and sugar in a bowl and mix well. Combine the milk, eggs and oil in a small bowl and mix well. Add to the cornmeal mixture and mix well.

Spoon the chicken mixture into a 9×13-inch baking pan. Pour the cornmeal mixture over the chicken mixture, sealing to the edges. Bake at 400 degrees for 30 minutes or until the crust is light golden brown.

YIELD: 6 TO 8 SERVINGS

NANCY KAMMAN
STATION 7

Physco Cichon's Crispy Baked Chicken

1 (2½- TO 3-POUND) CHICKEN
1 CUP SKIM MILK
1 CUP CORNFLAKE CRUMBS
1 TEASPOON ROSEMARY
½ TEASPOON FRESHLY GROUND PEPPER

Line a baking pan with foil and spray lightly with nonstick cooking spray. Cut the chicken into pieces. Remove the skin and fat.

Pour the milk into a shallow dish. Combine the cornflake crumbs, rosemary and pepper in a shallow dish and mix well. Dip each chicken piece into the milk and then into the cornflake crumb mixture. Arrange the chicken in the prepared pan so pieces do not touch.

Bake at 400 degrees for 45 minutes or until cooked through.

YIELD: 4 SERVINGS

STEVEN CICHON
STATION 28

Home of the "77 Sunset
Strip—Attitude is
Everything" firefighter BBQ
Team, Station 77 houses a
ladder, engine, ambulance,
and evacuation boat.
Opened in 1990, the west-
side station serves the
Spring Branch community
off Interstate 10 West.

"Driving You Crazy" Baked Chicken and Rice

2 CHICKEN BREASTS, ABOUT
   1½ POUNDS
1 (5-OUNCE) PACKAGE
   BROWN AND WILD RICE
   OR LONG GRAIN AND
   WILD RICE
1½ CUPS WATER

¼ CUP DRY WHITE WINE OR
   WATER
1 (9- OR 10-OUNCE) PACKAGE
   FROZEN NO-SALT-ADDED
   PEAS
¾ TEASPOON ITALIAN
   SEASONING

Cut each chicken breast into halves lengthwise. Remove the
skin and fat.

Combine the rice and water in a 2-quart baking dish,
discarding the rice seasoning packet. Stir in the wine, peas and
Italian seasoning. Arrange the chicken over the rice mixture.

Bake, covered, for 1 hour or until chicken and rice are tender.

YIELD: 4 SERVINGS   STEVE NEWSOME
                                        STATION 93

Teriyaki Chicken

1 (10-OUNCE) BOTTLE TERIYAKI
   SAUCE
1 (8-OUNCE) BOTTLE ITALIAN
   SALAD DRESSING

2 POUNDS BONELESS SKINLESS
   CHICKEN BREASTS

Combine the teriyaki sauce and salad dressing in a bowl and
mix well. Arrange the chicken in a single layer in a shallow dish.
Pour the teriyaki mixture over the chicken. Marinate, covered,
in the refrigerator for 2 to 3 hours. Drain the chicken, discarding
the marinade.

Place on a grill over hot coals. Grill until tender and cooked
through, turning once. Serve with mixed vegetables, wild rice
and wheat rolls.

YIELD: 8 SERVINGS   TERRY VICK
                                        STATION 77

Station 75's Italian Chicken

8 ROMANO TOMATOES

1 LARGE WHITE ONION

4 TO 5 TABLESPOONS OLIVE OIL

1 CUP WHITE WINE

3 TABLESPOONS MINCED GARLIC

2 TABLESPOONS OREGANO

OLIVE OIL

4 BONELESS SKINLESS CHICKEN
    BREASTS

ITALIAN SEASONED BREAD
    CRUMBS

4 SLICES PROVOLONE CHEESE

8 OUNCES SPAGHETTI

1 CUP (2 STICKS) MARGARINE

1 BUNCH PARSLEY, CHOPPED

Peel, seed and chop the tomatoes. Chop the onion. Heat 4 to 5 tablespoons olive oil in a large skillet over low heat. Add the tomatoes and onion. Add the wine. Bring to a simmer. Stir in the garlic and oregano. Cook for 2 hours, stirring occasionally.

Brush olive oil over the chicken. Dredge in the bread crumbs to coat. Place on a baking sheet. Bake at 375 degrees for 45 minutes or until cooked through. Place a slice of provolone cheese over each chicken breast. Let stand until melted.

Cook the spaghetti using the package directions; drain. Heat the margarine in a skillet until melted. Stir in the parsley. Combine the spaghetti and margarine mixture in a large bowl and mix well.

Serve the spaghetti mixture with the chicken. Spoon the tomato sauce over each.

YIELD: 4 SERVINGS

DAVID MCBROOM
STATION 75

POULTRY

Fire Station 75

In the heartbeat of suburban Houston, this neighborhood-oriented fire station on Dairy Ashford has a pulse for activities in the west memorial area. During the holidays, Station 75 will not be outdone on their Christmas decorations and are expected to carry Santa Claus safely through the neighborhood. They are active in community activities at the nearby West Houston Medical Center and open their doors to hundreds of children annually. Once they even delivered a baby. Equipped with an engine, ladder, and a Medic unit, Station 75 is a full house. Additionally, HFD's Rescue Team practices rappelling at the drill tower.

Stir-Fry Vegetables over Pasta

10 POUNDS CHICKEN LEG
    QUARTERS
1 (3-POUND) PACKAGE FROZEN
    MIXED VEGETABLES
SALT AND PEPPER TO TASTE
GARLIC TO TASTE

½ CUP COLD WATER
3 TABLESPOONS CORNSTARCH
½ CUP (ABOUT) SOY SAUCE
2 TO 3 POUNDS ANGEL HAIR
    PASTA

Combine the chicken with enough water to cover. Bring to a boil. Boil until the chicken is tender and cooked through. Remove the chicken, reserving ½ cup of the broth. Chop the chicken, discarding the skin and bones.

Stir-fry the vegetables in the reserved broth in a skillet. Add the salt, pepper and garlic. Combine the cold water and cornstarch in a small bowl and mix until smooth. Stir the cornstarch mixture and soy sauce into the vegetables. Cook until the mixture is thickened, stirring frequently. Add the chicken, mixing well.

Cook the pasta using the package directions; drain. Serve the vegetable mixture over the pasta. Serve with homemade bread.

NOTE: Most firefighters come to the fire station to escape the diet their wives put them on. You feed them this and they don't realize they are eating healthy food. Just don't let them eat more than three or four slices of homemade bread.

YIELD: 10 TO 12 SERVINGS

MIKE A. GIRARDI
STATION 93

POULTRY

Hawaiian Chicken

2 PACKAGES CHICKEN WINGS, OR
  8 OR 9 CHICKEN BREASTS
SALT AND PEPPER
1 (16-OUNCE) CAN PINEAPPLE
  CHUNKS

½ CUP PACKED BROWN SUGAR
2 TABLESPOONS CORNSTARCH
2 TABLESPOONS MILK
1 (8-OUNCE) JAR PICANTE SAUCE

Sprinkle the chicken with salt and pepper. Arrange in a shallow baking pan. Bake at 350 degrees until the chicken is brown on all sides.

Drain the pineapple, reserving the juice. Combine the reserved juice, brown sugar, cornstarch and milk in a bowl and mix until smooth. Stir in the pineapple. Spoon over the chicken. Bake for 10 to 15 minutes or until the sauce is slightly thickened.

Pour the picante sauce over the chicken mixture. Bake, covered with foil, until heated through and the chicken is tender. Serve with scalloped potatoes and green beans.

NOTE: This recipe has been shared among fire stations and it is a favorite at Station 68 on the C shift.

YIELD: 8 OR 9 SERVINGS

MIKE HUTCHENS
STATION 10

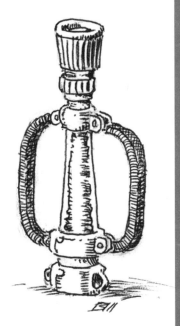

Fire Station 10

When arriving at the fire station in the morning, one of the first priorities is planning the day's meals. At fire station 10, this was not always an easy task. Firefighter Michael Hutchens got tired of hearing, "I don't know," so he came up with an organized plan. He created an in-house cookbook, *Firehouse Feasts*, listing a shopping list and numbering the recipes. So now the decision lies with the "fill-in." They pick a number and that determines the menu for the day. Nicknamed "Best in the West," Station 10 responds to a predominately Asian community. Even the number "10" is translated in Vietnamese on the firehouse. Ambulance 10 is among the top-three busiest in the city, and Engine 10 ranks in the top 20.

Fried Turkey

1 (12- TO 13-POUND) TURKEY
ITALIAN SALAD DRESSING
2 TABLESPOONS GARLIC JUICE
2 TABLESPOONS CRAB BOIL
  POWDER

1 TABLESPOON
  WORCESTERSHIRE SAUCE
1 TABLESPOON ONION POWDER
1 TEASPOON CAYENNE PEPPER
PEANUT OIL FOR FRYING

Place the turkey in a Cajun cooker. Add water to the cooker until it is 2 to 3 inches above the turkey. Remove the turkey and pat dry. Mark the spot where the top of the water is. Pour out the water.

Strain the salad dressing. Combine the garlic juice, crab boil, Worcestershire sauce, onion powder and cayenne pepper in a 1 cup measure. Add enough salad dressing to measure 1 cup and mix well. Inject the salad dressing mix into the breast, thigh, leg and wing areas of the turkey until the area rises slightly using a Cajun long stem injector. Chill, covered, for 8 to 12 hours.

Let the turkey stand at room temperature for 1 hour. Pour peanut oil into the cooker to the mark. Heat to 325 to 350 degrees. Insert the turkey into the cooker slowly; oil will splatter. Cook for 3½ to 4 minutes per pound. Remove and set turkey over a paper-towel-lined container to drain; let stand for 5 minutes.

YIELD: 25 TO 30 SERVINGS

LOUIS S. MOORE
CAPTAIN, EMERGENCY OPERATIONS

2-Alarm Turkey Spaghetti

2 (26-OUNCE) CANS ROASTED
    GARLIC SPAGHETTI SAUCE
½ YELLOW ONION, CHOPPED
1 TABLESPOON SUGAR
1 TEASPOON OREGANO OR
    ITALIAN SEASONING

1 TEASPOON PARSLEY
2 POUNDS GROUND TURKEY
WINE TO TASTE
16 OUNCES SPAGHETTI

Combine the spaghetti sauce, onion, sugar, oregano and parsley in a large pot and mix well. Cook, covered, over low heat.

Brown the turkey in a skillet, stirring until crumbly; drain. Stir into the sauce. Stir in the wine. Cover and bring to a simmer.

Cook the spaghetti using the package directions; drain. Serve the spaghetti with the sauce.

NOTE: Caution: Rookies are to be kept out of the kitchen during food preparation and away from sharp objects.

YIELD: 8 TO 10 SERVINGS

STEVE E. KRAMER
STATION 96

Fire Station 96

In January 1994, the city of Houston annexed the far Houston northwest Willowbrook area. Initial crews at Station 96 were quartered in what the members coined "a frozen food locker." The only difference was it included two bunk beds, a couch, and a sink. Eventually, this was replaced with a trailer, their new home for six years. In March 2000, a new building was opened on Willowchase Drive, near Willowbrook Mall. With a new tower ladder truck, the crews have adopted an unofficial policy that anyone accidentally hitting a curb while driving this tremendous vehicle will have to buy all members a Coke.

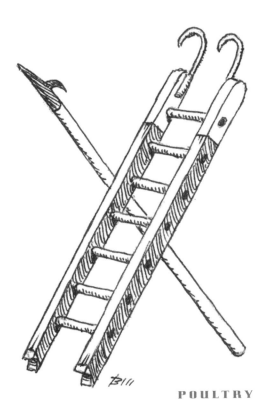

Original Turkey Burgers

1 POUND GROUND TURKEY

1 (6-OUNCE) JAR MARINATED
ARTICHOKE HEARTS,
COARSELY CHOPPED

2 MARINATED BELL PEPPERS,
COARSELY CHOPPED

2 SLICES YELLOW ONION, FINELY
CHOPPED

8 OUNCES FETA CHEESE,
CRUMBLED

2 CARROTS, FINELY CHOPPED

2 RIBS CELERY, FINELY CHOPPED

2 GREEN ONIONS, FINELY
CHOPPED

1 (4-OUNCE) CAN CHOPPED
BLACK OLIVES

SALT AND PEPPER TO TASTE

1/4 CUP BREAD CRUMBS

Combine the turkey, artichoke hearts, bell peppers, onion, feta cheese, carrots, celery, green onions and olives in a large bowl and mix well. Add the salt, pepper and bread crumbs and mix well. Shape into 4 patties.

Spray a grill rack with nonstick cooking spray. Place the patties on the grill rack over hot coals. Grill until cooked through, turning once. Serve on buns with honey mustard, tomatoes and lettuce.

YIELD: 4 SERVINGS

TERRY LITZINGER
STATION 75

Fancy Clam Spaghetti

SPAGHETTI

1/3 CUP OLIVE OIL

1 TABLESPOON (HEAPING)
   FINELY CHOPPED GARLIC

2 TEASPOONS OREGANO

2 TEASPOONS BASIL

2 (7-OUNCE) CANS CHOPPED
   CLAMS

1 CUP SLICED MUSHROOMS
   (OPTIONAL)

1/4 CUP WHITE WINE (OPTIONAL)

SALT AND PEPPER TO TASTE

GRATED PARMESAN OR ROMANO
   CHEESE

FRESH PARSLEY SPRIGS

Cook the spaghetti using the package directions; drain. Set aside and keep warm.

Heat the olive oil in a skillet over medium heat. Add the garlic, oregano and basil. Cook for 1 to 2 minutes, stirring frequently. Drain 1 can of the clams. Add the drained clams, undrained clams and mushrooms to the garlic mixture. Bring to a boil. Stir in the wine. Reduce the heat. Simmer, covered, for 5 minutes. Season with salt and pepper. Add additional wine or a small amount of water to make of the desired consistency.

Place the spaghetti in a serving bowl. Spoon the clam sauce over the spaghetti. Sprinkle with Parmesan cheese. Garnish with parsley sprigs.

You may substitute the drained liquid from the clams or 1/4 cup water for the wine. You may add 2 tablespoons tomato paste for a red clam sauce. You may substitute 1/2 to 1 cup chopped shrimp, crab meat or scallops or a combination for the clams.

NOTE: This is a very quick and easy recipe. It does not require a long preparation time and can be fixed beforehand and reheated quickly. Suggested side dishes are a tossed green salad and toasted garlic bread.

YIELD: VARIABLE

PAT BROWN
SYSTEMS DEVELOPMENT

Crab and Shrimp Fondue

16 OUNCES CREAM CHEESE	2 DROPS OF TABASCO SAUCE
1 CUP SOUR CREAM	½ TEASPOON DRY MUSTARD
1 (10-OUNCE) CAN CREAM OF	3 TABLESPOONS SHERRY
SHRIMP SOUP	1 (7-OUNCE) CAN CRAB MEAT
½ TEASPOON SALT	1 (4-OUNCE) CAN SHRIMP
⅛ TEASPOON GARLIC POWDER	FRENCH BREAD, CUBED

Combine the cream cheese, sour cream, soup, salt, garlic powder, Tabasco sauce, mustard and sherry in a saucepan. Cook until smooth and heated through, stirring constantly. Stir in the crab meat and shrimp. Cook until the crab meat and shrimp are heated through. Spoon into a fondue pot. Serve with French bread.

YIELD: 2 TO 4 SERVINGS

KENNETH M. BOLES
STATION 103

Crawfish Étouffée

1 GREEN BELL PEPPER, CHOPPED	1 (12-OUNCE) CAN TOMATO
1 LARGE ONION, CHOPPED	PASTE
3 OR 4 RIBS CELERY, CHOPPED	1 POUND SHRIMP, SHELLED
1 CUP (2 STICKS) MARGARINE	1 POUND CRAWFISH, SHELLED
1 (10-OUNCE) CAN TOMATOES	1 TEASPOON CHOPPED GARLIC
WITH GREEN PEPPERS	TONY CHACHERE'S ORIGINAL
2 (10-OUNCE) CANS CREAM OF	SEASONING TO TASTE
MUSHROOM SOUP	HOT COOKED RICE

Sauté the bell pepper, onion and celery in the margarine in a skillet until tender. Combine with the tomatoes, soup, tomato paste, shrimp, crawfish, garlic and Tony Chachere's Original Seasoning in a 5-quart pot. Bring to a simmer. Simmer for 2 to 4 hours. Serve over hot cooked rice.

YIELD: 6 TO 8 SERVINGS

RICHARD MANN
STATION 10

Cajun Crawfish Pasta

2 TABLESPOONS OLIVE OIL
3 GARLIC CLOVES, CHOPPED
3 SCALLIONS, CHOPPED
½ BELL PEPPER, CHOPPED
1 POUND CRAWFISH TAILS OR
  SHRIMP
1 ROMA TOMATO, CHOPPED
2 TABLESPOONS FLOUR
2 CUPS MILK

1 TABLESPOON TONY
  CHACHERE'S ORIGINAL
  SEASONING, OR TO TASTE
1 TEASPOON SALT
1 TEASPOON PEPPER
¾ CUP GRATED PARMESAN
  CHEESE
16 OUNCES HOT COOKED
  LINGUINI

Heat a large skillet over medium heat. Add the olive oil. Add the garlic and sauté for 1 minute. Add the scallions and bell pepper. Sauté for 3 minutes. Add the crawfish and tomato. Sauté for 2 minutes. Stir in the flour. Stir in the milk. Add the Tony Chachere's Original Seasoning, salt and pepper and mix well. Cook until thickened, stirring constantly. Stir in the Parmesan cheese. Serve over the linguini.

YIELD: 4 TO 6 SERVINGS

KELLY BOST-CHANDLER
HUMAN RESOURCES

Firehouse Shrimp

1 POUND BACON STRIPS
2 GREEN ONIONS
1 MEDIUM WHITE ONION
2 BELL PEPPERS
FILÉ POWDER
1 (4-OUNCE) JAR CHOPPED
    MUSHROOMS
1 POUND SMALL OR MEDIUM
    SHRIMP, PEELED, DEVEINED
SALT AND PEPPER TO TASTE

Fry the bacon in a skillet until crisp. Remove to paper towels to drain, reserving the drippings in the skillet. Crumble the bacon.

Chop the green onions, white onion and bell peppers. Add to the bacon drippings. Cook until tender, stirring frequently. Stir in enough filé powder to make of the desired consistency and the undrained mushrooms. Cook, covered, for 10 minutes, adding water and filé powder as needed to make of the desired consistency.

Stir the shrimp into the bell pepper mixture. Cook for 3 to 5 minutes. Stir in the bacon. Cook for 2 to 3 minutes. Season with salt and pepper. Serve over hot cooked white rice.

YIELD: 6 TO 8 SERVINGS

LESTER TYRA
FIRE CHIEF

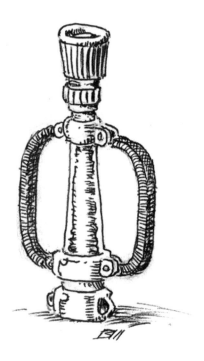

Station 71's Shrimp Alfredo

1 (10-OUNCE) PACKAGE FROZEN
    CAULIFLOWER, WATER
    CHESTNUTS, BROCCOLI AND
    CARROTS
16 OUNCES ANGEL HAIR PASTA

1 TO 2 POUNDS SHRIMP, PEELED,
    DEVEINED
1 (16-OUNCE) JAR ALFREDO
    SAUCE

Cook the vegetables using the package directions; drain. Cook the pasta using the package directions; drain.

Combine the vegetables, shrimp and sauce in a saucepan. Bring to a simmer. Simmer for 5 minutes. Serve over the pasta.

NOTE: This recipe is enjoyed by Station 71 mainly because it's very quickly made and is filling. Together with a salad and rolls, dinner is ready in no time.

YIELD: 4 TO 8 SERVINGS

GARY BENNETT AND RONALD GRIMSTEAD
STATION 71

Fire Station 71

Station 71 went from living out of an L-shaped trailer for about 13 years to an ex-funeral home shared with the Houston Police Department before they moved into their present building in 1992. This is the district station for Clear Lake. Housed at this station is an ambulance, ladder, and a truck.

Blackened Redfish

4 REDFISH FILLETS
½ CUP (1 STICK) BUTTER

BLACKENED REDFISH
SEASONING

Cut each fillet into 3 thin pieces. Place the butter in a shallow microwave-safe dish. Microwave until melted.

Heat a cast-iron skillet until very hot. Coat a redfish piece with the melted butter on both sides. Place in the skillet; this will produce a lot of smoke. Sprinkle the blackened redfish seasoning over the fish. Cook for 45 to 60 seconds; turn. Sprinkle the blackened redfish seasoning over the fish. Cook for 45 to 60 seconds or until the fish flakes easily. Repeat with the remaining fish pieces. Serve immediately.

YIELD: 12 SERVINGS   STATION 81

Creole Quickie

CHOPPED ONIONS
CHOPPED BELL PEPPERS
CHOPPED CELERY
SLICED SAUSAGE
MARGARINE
SHRIMP
CRAB MEAT

CRAWFISH
TOMATO SAUCE
DICED TOMATOES WITH GREEN
CHILES
STEWED TOMATOES
GARLIC POWDER

Sauté the onions, bell peppers, celery and sausage in margarine in a skillet until tender. Add the shrimp, crab meat, crawfish, tomato sauce, diced tomatoes, stewed tomatoes and garlic powder and mix well. Simmer, covered, for 40 minutes or until all ingredients are cooked through, stirring occasionally. Serve over hot cooked rice.

NOTE: The amount of ingredients varies depending upon how many firefighters you want to serve.

YIELD: VARIABLE   DIANA FAYE STEWARD
                                                     FIRE PERMITS

Baked Fish and Dressing

¼ PACKAGE LOUISIANA SHRIMP
    AND CRAB BOIL, OR TO TASTE
1 POUND SHRIMP, PEELED
1 (16-OUNCE) JAR OYSTERS,
    DRAINED
4 (6-OUNCE) PACKAGES CORN
    BREAD STUFFING MIX

8 OUNCES CRAB MEAT
7 LARGE FRESH FISH FILLETS
1 CUP (2 STICKS) BUTTER,
    MELTED
JUICE OF 1 LEMON
SALT AND PEPPER TO TASTE

Bring enough water to cover the shrimp and oysters to a boil in a saucepan. Add the shrimp and crab boil, shrimp and oysters. Boil for 3 minutes or until shrimp is white. Drain; reserving the broth. Chop the shrimp and oysters.

Prepare the stuffing using the package directions and substituting the reserved broth for the water. Add the shrimp, oysters and crab meat and mix well.

Cut the fish into halves horizontally if they are thick enough. Combine half the butter, half the lemon juice, salt and pepper in a baking pan and mix well. Arrange enough of the fish over the bottom of the pan to cover, coating both sides of the fish with the butter mixture.

Combine the remaining butter, remaining lemon juice, salt and pepper in a shallow dish. Coat both sides of the remaining fish in the butter mixture. Layer the stuffing and remaining fish over the fish layer ½ at a time.

Bake at 375 degrees for 45 minutes. Broil for 10 minutes. Serve with new potatoes and corn on the cob boiled in Louisiana Boil.

NOTE: This is an unbelievable dish. The key is to use fresh fish.

YIELD: 9 SERVINGS

EDWARD JOHNSON
STATION 45

Fire Station 45

Station 45 prides itself on the ability of all four shifts to get along so well. At some fire stations where competition among shifts is common, each shift stocks their own refrigerator and keeps it locked when they are not on duty. Not at Station 45. This northeast Houston fire station has managed to get away with sharing food among shifts—with the exception of some frozen items.

"Dropping is a Good Thing" Salmon Potato Croquettes

12 OUNCES POTATO, PEELED, SHREDDED

18 OUNCES COOKED FLAKED SALMON

2 EGGS, BEATEN

4 EGG WHITES, BEATEN

¼ CUP GRATED ONION

2 TABLESPOONS LEMON JUICE

2 TEASPOONS WORCESTERSHIRE SAUCE

2 OUNCES PARMESAN CHEESE, GRATED

1 TEASPOON GRATED LEMON ZEST

1 TEASPOON CAYENNE PEPPER

1 TABLESPOON DILL

Bring enough water to cover the shredded potato to a boil in a saucepan. Add the potato. Boil for 1 minute; drain.

Combine the potato, salmon, eggs, egg whites, onion, lemon juice, Worcestershire sauce, Parmesan cheese, lemon zest, cayenne pepper and dill in a bowl and mix well. Shape into patties.

Cook the croquettes on a nonstick skillet or griddle sprayed with nonstick cooking spray until brown on both sides. Serve with sour cream, cocktail sauce, horseradish and lemon wedges.

YIELD: 8 SERVINGS

LARRY MCCLURE
STATION 31

Grilled Blackfin Tuna

4 (6-OUNCE) ½-INCH-THICK
  BLACKFIN TUNA STEAKS OR
  SKINLESS FILLETS

ITALIAN SALAD DRESSING
SALT AND PEPPER TO TASTE
LEMONS, CUT INTO WEDGES

Place the tuna in a nonreactive bowl. Pour enough salad dressing over the tuna to cover. Marinate, covered, in the refrigerator for 3 hours or longer. Drain the tuna and discard the marinade.

Place the tuna on a grill over hot coals. Grill for 5 to 10 minutes or until the tuna flakes easily, basting with Italian salad dressing and turning once.

Season with salt and pepper. Serve with the lemon wedges. You may substitute any other firm fish, such as shark, for the tuna.

NOTE: We like this dish for two reasons: It is low in fat and it requires a fishing trip! (Station 27A refuses to buy fish!)

YIELD: 4 SERVINGS   STATION 27

Fire Station 27

Station 27 is the oldest station still in operation. Still working out of its original building, this station was built in 1940. A former member of the station includes a Dalmatian named Virgil who died in 1950. His gravesite is in front of the station. Located one block north of Interstate 10 East, Station 27 serves the predominately Hispanic and African-American communities of Denver Harbor and parts of the Fifth Ward.

Noodles Delight

1 (16-OUNCE) PACKAGE NOODLES
4 SLICES CHEESE
2 TABLESPOONS MARGARINE
2 (6-OUNCE) CANS MEXICAN CORN, DRAINED
2 (6-OUNCE) CANS TUNA, CUT INTO PIECES
1 (20-OUNCE) CAN PINEAPPLE CHUNKS, DRAINED

Cook the noodles using the package directions; drain. Place on a large microwave-safe plate. Arrange the slices of cheese over the noodles.

Combine the margarine and corn in a saucepan. Cook until the margarine is melted and the corn is heated through. Spoon over the cheese.

Arrange the tuna and pineapple around the noodles. Microwave for 2 minutes. Serve immediately.

YIELD: 3 OR 4 SERVINGS

DIANA FAYE STEWARD
FIRE PERMITS

Penne all' Arrabbiata

½ CUP FINELY CHOPPED DRIED
    PANCETTA
3 GARLIC CLOVES, MINCED
½ RIB CELERY, MINCED
1 SMALL ONION, MINCED
¼ CUP EXTRA-VIRGIN
    OLIVE OIL
4 FRESH BASIL LEAVES, TORN

2 CUPS CHOPPED PEELED
    TOMATOES
½ TEASPOON CRUSHED CHILES
SALT AND FRESHLY GROUND
    PEPPER
14 OUNCES PENNE PASTA
2 TABLESPOONS GRATED
    PECORINO CHEESE

Brown the pancetta, garlic, celery and onion in the olive oil in a skillet. Add the basil, tomatoes and chiles and mix well. Season with salt and pepper. Simmer over medium-low heat for 20 minutes or until the tomatoes and oil begin to separate.

Cook the penne in salted water using the package directions until al dente; drain. Add to the sauce. Cook over high heat for 2 to 3 minutes, stirring constantly. Sprinkle with the pecorino cheese.

YIELD: 4 SERVINGS

DAVID PERSSE
MEDICAL DIRECTOR

"Relief Time" Nachos Pizza

6 CORN TORTILLAS
8 OUNCES SHREDDED REDUCED-
    FAT CHEDDAR CHEESE
1 (10-OUNCE) CAN TOMATOES
    WITH HOT GREEN CHILES

8 OUNCES SHREDDED REDUCED-
    FAT MOZZARELLA CHEESE
FAT-FREE SOUR CREAM

Overlap the tortillas to form a circle in a baking dish. Sprinkle the Cheddar cheese over the tortillas. Spoon the tomatoes over the Cheddar cheese. Sprinkle the mozzarella cheese over the tomatoes. Broil on medium-high until the cheese melts and the edges of the tortillas are light brown and crisp. Spread the sour cream over the top. Cut into 8 slices.

YIELD: 4 SERVINGS

LARRY MCCLURE
STATION 31

About the EMS Division

In 1971, the Houston Fire Department began providing quality emergency medical care. Our highly educated EMS personnel pursue excellence in their profession by combining the benefits of medical science with the art of compassionate care. In all cases, potential patients are approached with the greatest professionalism and concern for their well-being.

Pasta with Cream Sauce

2 TABLESPOONS (HEAPING) MINCED GARLIC	2 CUPS HEAVY CREAM
1 TABLESPOON BASIL	2 POUNDS RIGATONI PASTA
1 TABLESPOON PARSLEY	2 CUPS GRATED PARMESAN CHEESE
½ CUP (1 STICK) BUTTER	SALT AND PEPPER TO TASTE

Sauté the garlic, basil and parsley in the butter in a skillet. Stir in the cream. Cook until heated through.

Cook the pasta using the package directions; drain. Place in a large bowl. Pour the cream sauce over the pasta. Sprinkle the cheese over the top. Season with salt and pepper.

YIELD: 8 SERVINGS — DISTRICT 26

Spinach-Stuffed Shells

2 (16-OUNCE) PACKAGES MANICOTTI SHELLS	6 CUPS COTTAGE CHEESE
2 (10-OUNCE) PACKAGES FROZEN CHOPPED SPINACH, THAWED	2 EGGS
16 OUNCES MOZZARELLA CHEESE, SHREDDED	2 TEASPOONS GARLIC POWDER
	1 TEASPOON PEPPER
	2 (32-OUNCE) JARS VEGETABLE-STYLE SPAGHETTI SAUCE

Cook the pasta shells using the package directions; drain. Drain the spinach, pressing out the excess moisture. Combine the spinach, mozzarella cheese, cottage cheese, eggs, garlic powder and pepper and mix well. Spoon into the manicotti shells.

Spread a thin layer of spaghetti sauce over the bottoms of two 9×13-inch baking pans. Arrange the stuffed shells in a single layer over the sauce. Spoon the remaining sauce over the shells. Bake, covered with foil, at 375 degrees for 35 minutes.

YIELD: 6 TO 8 SERVINGS — BOB PARRY EMS

Vegetarian Spaghetti

3 BUNCHES GREEN ONIONS, SLICED

¼ CUP OLIVE OIL

1 POUND WHOLE TOMATOES, SLICED

8 OUNCES FRESH MUSHROOMS, SLICED

2 GREEN BELL PEPPERS, CUT INTO 16 PIECES

1 RED BELL PEPPER, CUT INTO 8 PIECES

2 ZUCCHINI, CUT INTO ½-INCH-THICK SLICES

¼ CUP OLIVE OIL

2 TABLESPOONS OREGANO

2 TABLESPOONS BASIL

1 TABLESPOON GARLIC POWDER

1 TABLESPOON TONY CHACHERE'S ORIGINAL SEASONING

2 (6-OUNCE) CANS TOMATO PASTE

2 (8-OUNCE) CANS TOMATO SAUCE

1 CUP WATER

SPAGHETTI, ELBOW MACARONI OR SHELL MACARONI

Sauté the green onions in ¼ cup olive oil in a skillet. Add the tomatoes, mushrooms, bell peppers and zucchini. Stir in ¼ cup olive oil. Stir in the oregano, basil, garlic powder and Tony Chachere's Original Seasoning. Add the tomato paste, tomato sauce and water and mix well. Cook over medium-low heat for 1 hour, adding additional water to make of the desired consistency.

Cook the spaghetti using the package directions; drain. Rinse with cool water. Combine the spaghetti and sauce in a large bowl and mix well.

NOTE: Firefighters are amazed at how good this is because there is no meat!

YIELD: VARIABLE

FRANK W. GRIZZAFFI
EMERGENCY OPERATIONS

WELL, THAT FIGURES!!
ROOKIE FIREFIGHTER: ROOKIE COOK!!

Ambrosia of the Gods

1 (16-OUNCE) CAN CHUNK
    PINEAPPLE
1 (8-OUNCE) CAN CRUSHED
    PINEAPPLE
1 (4-OUNCE) PACKAGE PISTACHIO
    INSTANT PUDDING MIX
1 CUP CHOPPED WALNUTS OR
    PECANS

1 CUP SHREDDED COCONUT
12 TO 16 OUNCES WHIPPED
    TOPPING
1 CUP MINIATURE
    MARSHMALLOWS

Combine the chunk pineapple and crushed pineapple in a bowl and mix well. Sprinkle the pudding mix over the top. Let stand for 3 to 5 minutes.

Combine the walnuts and coconut in a bowl and mix well. Add to the pineapple mixture and mix well. Stir in the whipped topping. Add the marshmallows and mix well. Chill, covered, for 2 hours or longer.

YIELD: 10 TO 12 SERVINGS

BEN BRYMER
EMERGENCY OPERATIONS

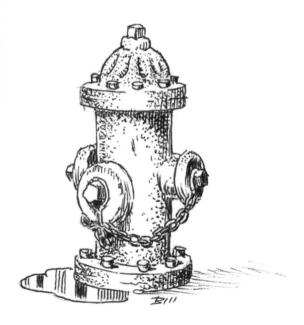

Apricot Bread Pudding

⅓ TO ½ CUP SUGAR-FREE
    APRICOT FRUIT SPREAD
6 (½-INCH-THICK) SLICES
    FRENCH BREAD
1 CUP EGG SUBSTITUTE

1 (12-OUNCE) CAN EVAPORATED
    SKIM MILK
¼ CUP PACKED LIGHT BROWN
    SUGAR
1 TEASPOON VANILLA EXTRACT

Spread the fruit spread over one side of each bread slice. Cut the bread slices into 1-inch squares. Layer the squares fruit side up in a 1½-quart baking dish coated with butter-flavor nonstick cooking spray.

Whisk the egg substitute in a bowl until light and fluffy. Whisk in the evaporated milk, brown sugar and vanilla. Pour over the bread slices. Let stand for 30 minutes.

Bake at 350 degrees for 1 hour or until a knife inserted in the center comes out clean and the pudding has risen and is dry on top.

YIELD: 4 TO 6 SERVINGS

MICHAEL S. PLUMMER
FIRE ALARM

DESSERTS

155

Super D Banana Pudding

1 (6-OUNCE) PACKAGE VANILLA
   INSTANT PUDDING MIX
1 (4-OUNCE) PACKAGE BANANA
   CREAM INSTANT PUDDING MIX
3 OUNCES CREAM CHEESE,
   SOFTENED

8 OUNCES WHIPPED TOPPING
VANILLA WAFERS
1 BUNCH BANANAS, SLICED

Prepare the pudding mixes together using the package directions and decreasing the milk by 1 cup. Let stand until thickened. Add the cream cheese and mix until smooth. Fold in the whipped topping.

Layer the vanilla wafers, pudding mixture and bananas alternately in a dish until all ingredients are used. Chill, covered, for 4 hours or longer.

You may double the pudding amounts, use 8 ounces of cream cheese and 16 ounces of whipped topping to increase the number of servings.

YIELD: 8 TO 10 SERVINGS

GREG COLLINS
ARSON

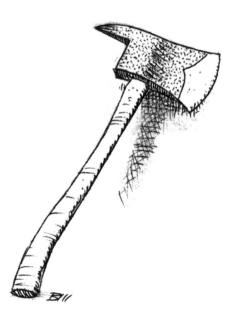

Banana Split Cake

½ CUP (1 STICK) MARGARINE

2 CUPS GRAHAM CRACKER
  CRUMBS

1 CUP (2 STICKS) MARGARINE,
  SOFTENED

2 CUPS CONFECTIONERS' SUGAR

2 EGGS

1 (15-OUNCE) CAN CRUSHED
  PINEAPPLE, DRAINED

4 BANANAS, SLICED

9 OUNCES WHIPPED TOPPING

CHOPPED NUTS

1 (4-OUNCE) JAR MARASCHINO
  CHERRIES, DRAINED

Heat ½ cup margarine in a saucepan until melted. Add the graham cracker crumbs and mix well. Press over the bottom of a dessert dish.

Beat 1 cup margarine, confectioners' sugar and eggs in a mixing bowl for 15 minutes. Pour over the graham cracker crust. Arrange the pineapple and bananas over the confectioners' sugar mixture. Spread the whipped topping over the fruit, sealing to the edges.

Sprinkle the nuts and cherries over the top. Chill, covered, in the refrigerator.

NOTE: To avoid raw eggs that may carry salmonella, we suggest using an equivalent amount of egg substitute.

YIELD: 6 TO 8 SERVINGS

GRETCHEN WOLF
STATION 12

Blueberry and Pineapple Crunch

1 (20-OUNCE) CAN CRUSHED
    PINEAPPLE
1 (21-OUNCE) CAN BLUEBERRY
    PIE FILLING
1 (2-LAYER) PACKAGE YELLOW
    CAKE MIX

½ CUP (1 STICK) BUTTER,
    MELTED
2 CUPS CHOPPED WALNUTS

Drain the pineapple. Spread over the bottom of a 9×13-inch baking pan. Spread the pie filling over the pineapple. Sprinkle the cake mix over the pie filling, breaking up the lumps. Pour the butter over the cake mix. Sprinkle the walnuts over the top. Bake at 350 degrees for 35 to 45 minutes or until brown. Serve warm with vanilla ice cream.

YIELD: 10 TO 12 SERVINGS

MICHAEL GANN
RETIRED

Brooklyn Float

5 TABLESPOONS CHOCOLATE
    SYRUP
8 OUNCES SELTZER WATER,
    CHILLED

2 LARGE SCOOPS CHOCOLATE
    ICE CREAM

Pour the syrup into a large glass. Pour the seltzer water into the glass and stir 12 times or less. Add the ice cream. Serve with a straw and spoon.

YIELD: 1 SERVING

STEVE KRAMER
STATION 96

Captain Cobbler's Apple Crapple

1 CUP (2 STICKS) MARGARINE
3 CUPS SUGAR
3 CUPS FLOUR
1 TEASPOON BAKING POWDER

1¾ CUPS MILK
2 (21-OUNCE) CANS APPLE PIE
    FILLING
CINNAMON

Preheat the oven to 375 degrees. Melt the margarine in a cast-iron skillet in the oven. Combine the sugar, flour, baking powder and milk in a bowl and mix well. Add the melted margarine and mix well.

Pour half the batter into the skillet. Spoon the pie filling over the batter in the skillet. Pour the remaining batter over the pie filling. Bake for 50 to 60 minutes or until golden brown and set. Sprinkle cinnamon over the top. You may substitute any flavor of pie filling for the apple pie filling.

YIELD: 6 TO 8 SERVINGS

AL COGBILL
STATION 51

Captain Cogbill's Cobblers

Captain Cogbill or Captain Cobbler gets many requests for his famous cobblers, especially his apple crapple, as fellow firefighters have nicknamed it. If he makes it in the morning, it's usually gone by noon, except for the time he used salt instead of sugar. An easy mistake since the salt is stored next to the sugar in a large green bucket.

"I reached down underneath the cabinet and scooped into the salt by mistake," said Captain Cogbill. "When it came out of the oven it just didn't look right. The damage was already done so I didn't say anything."

Another firefighter took a big plate of it, hoping for the usual delicious cobbler. "I let him take a bite before I told him what happened," said Cogbill.

Cogbill hasn't lived this one down. His crew has never let him forget it. The C shift did remember to leave the cobbler for the oncoming shift. "They came in and naturally started eating it before we got up," said Cobbler.

Fast Firefighter Cobbler

1 (16-OUNCE) CAN SLICED
  PEACHES
1 (2-LAYER) PACKAGE WHITE
  CAKE MIX

½ CUP (1 STICK) BUTTER, SLICED

Spoon the peaches and juice over the bottom of a 9-inch baking pan. Sprinkle the cake mix over the peaches, breaking up any lumps. Place slices of butter over the cake mix. Bake at 350 degrees until brown. Serve with vanilla ice cream.

YIELD: 4 TO 6 SERVINGS

KEITH BOBBITT
STATION 11

Lazy Man Peach Cobbler

2 (16-OUNCE) CANS PEACHES,
  DRAINED
CINNAMON
1 (2-LAYER) PACKAGE YELLOW
  OR WHITE CAKE MIX

BUTTER OR MARGARINE, CUT
  INTO TEASPOON-SIZE PATS

Cut the peaches into small pieces. Arrange over the bottom of a 9×13-inch baking pan. Add enough water to cover the peaches. Sprinkle with cinnamon. Sprinkle the cake mix evenly over the cinnamon, breaking up any lumps. Sprinkle cinnamon over the cake mix. Place pats of butter close together over the top. Bake at 350 degrees for 1 hour.

YIELD: 10 SERVINGS

LARRY REISS
STATION 49

Cinnaberry Shortcake

1 ANGEL FOOD OR POUND CAKE

12 OUNCES WHIPPED TOPPING

2 TABLESPOONS (HEAPING)
    CINNAMON

2 (16-OUNCE) PACKAGES FROZEN
    STRAWBERRIES, THAWED

Cut the cake into halves lengthwise. Combine the whipped topping and cinnamon in a bowl and mix well. Drain the strawberries, reserving the juice.

Place one cake half in a bowl. Pour half the strawberry juice over the cake. Spoon half of the strawberries over the cake. Spread half of the cinnamon whipped topping over the strawberries. Repeat the layers with the remaining ingredients. Sprinkle additional cinnamon over the top. Chill, covered, in the refrigerator.

YIELD: 10 TO 12 SERVINGS

BOB PARRY
EMS

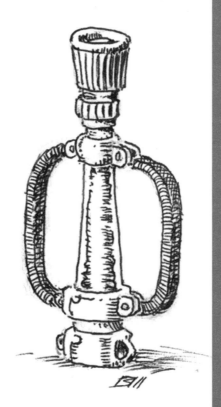

German Chocolate Cheesecake

1 (8-OUNCE) PACKAGE CHOCOLATE WAFERS, CRUSHED	1/4 TEASPOON SALT
	4 EGGS
	1/4 CUP EVAPORATED MILK
6 TABLESPOONS BUTTER, MELTED	1 (4-OUNCE) PACKAGE SWEET BAKING CHOCOLATE, MELTED
24 OUNCES CREAM CHEESE, SOFTENED	1 TEASPOON VANILLA EXTRACT
	GERMAN CHOCOLATE
1 1/4 CUPS SUGAR	CHEESECAKE TOPPING
3 TABLESPOONS CAKE FLOUR	(PAGE 163)

Combine the wafer crumbs and butter in a bowl and mix well. Press over the bottom and 1 3/4 inches up the side of a 9-inch springform pan.

Beat the cream cheese in a mixing bowl at medium speed until light and fluffy. Beat in the sugar, flour and salt gradually. Add the eggs 1 at a time, mixing well after each addition. Add the evaporated milk, chocolate and vanilla and mix well. Pour into the prepared crust.

Bake at 325 degrees for 1 hour. Let stand for 15 minutes. Loosen the cheesecake from the side of the pan with a knife. Let cool for 30 minutes. Remove the side of the pan. Spread the German Chocolate Cheesecake Topping over the top. Chill, covered, for 8 hours. Garnish with toasted shredded coconut, pecan halves and a chocolate curl in the center.

YIELD: 10 TO 12 SERVINGS

DONNIE MCCOMB
STATION 43

German Chocolate Cheesecake Topping

2 TEASPOONS CORNSTARCH
1¼ CUPS SUGAR
⅔ CUP EVAPORATED MILK
¼ CUP BUTTER, MELTED

¾ CUP CHOPPED PECANS
¾ CUP FLAKED COCONUT
1 TEASPOON VANILLA EXTRACT

Combine the cornstarch and sugar in a saucepan. Stir in the evaporated milk and butter. Bring to a boil over medium heat; boil until thickened, stirring constantly. Boil for 1 minute longer, stirring constantly. Remove from the heat. Stir in the pecans, coconut and vanilla. Let cool.

Dump Cake

1 (2-LAYER) PACKAGE YELLOW
   CAKE MIX
½ CUP (1 STICK) BUTTER
1 (8-OUNCE) CAN CRUSHED
   PINEAPPLE

1 (21-OUNCE) CAN CHERRY
   PIE FILLING

Sprinkle the cake mix over the bottom of a 9×9-inch baking pan. Cut the butter into pieces. Arrange the pieces over the cake mix.

Drain the pineapple. Combine the pineapple and pie filling in a bowl and mix well. Spread over the cake mix and butter in the prepared pan. Bake using the cake package instructions.

YIELD: 6 TO 8 SERVINGS

LARRY D. SMITH
FIRE ALARM

Greatest Thanksgiving Dessert Ever

1 (16-OUNCE) PACKAGE POUND
    CAKE MIX
1 EGG
2 TEASPOONS PUMPKIN PIE SPICE
2 TABLESPOONS MARGARINE,
    MELTED
8 OUNCES CREAM CHEESE,
    SOFTENED
1 (14-OUNCE) CAN SWEETENED
    CONDENSED MILK

2 EGGS
1 (16-OUNCE) CAN PUMPKIN
2 TEASPOONS PUMPKIN PIE SPICE
1/2 TEASPOON SALT
1/2 CUP CHOPPED PECANS
1/2 CUP CHOPPED WALNUTS
WHIPPED TOPPING

Combine the cake mix, 1 egg, 2 teaspoons pumpkin pie spice and margarine in a mixing bowl. Beat at low speed until crumbly. Press over the bottom of a 10×15-inch baking pan.

Beat the cream cheese in a mixing bowl until light and fluffy. Beat in the condensed milk, 2 eggs, 2 teaspoons pumpkin pie spice and salt gradually. Pour over the cake layer. Sprinkle the pecans and walnuts over the top.

Bake at 350 degrees for 30 minutes or until set. Let stand until cool. Chill, covered, in the refrigerator for 3 hours or longer. Cut into 48 bars. Top with whipped topping.

YIELD: 48 BARS

LARRY MCCLURE
STATION 31

Monkey Bread

1 CUP CHOPPED NUTS
MARASCHINO CHERRIES
1 CUP SUGAR
1 TABLESPOON CINNAMON

3 (8-COUNT) CANS BISCUITS
1 CUP PACKED BROWN SUGAR
½ CUP (1 STICK) BUTTER,
   MELTED

Grease a bundt pan. Sprinkle the nuts and cherries over the bottom of the pan.

Combine the sugar and cinnamon in a bowl and mix well. Cut each biscuit into 4 pieces. Roll each piece in the cinnamon sugar to coat. Arrange the coated biscuit pieces in the prepared pan. Combine the brown sugar and butter in a bowl and mix well. Pour over the biscuits.

Bake at 350 degrees for 35 to 40 minutes or until golden brown. Cool in the pan for 15 minutes. Invert onto a serving plate. Serve warm.

YIELD: 16 SERVINGS

GRETCHEN WOLF
STATION 12

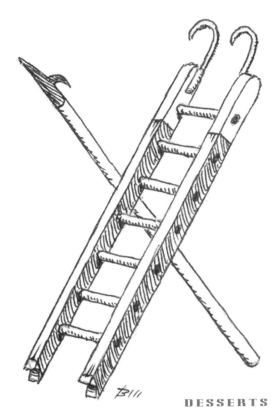

DESSERTS

165

Pineapple Bavarian Pudding

2 CUPS VANILLA COOKIE CRUMBS
¼ CUP (½ STICK) BUTTER, MELTED
1 (20-OUNCE) CAN PINEAPPLE TIDBITS
1 (3-OUNCE) PACKAGE VANILLA PUDDING AND PIE FILLING MIX
1 (3-OUNCE) PACKAGE LEMON GELATIN
4 OUNCES WHIPPED TOPPING

Combine the cookie crumbs and butter in a bowl and mix well. Press over the bottom of a 9×9-inch baking pan. Bake at 375 degrees for 8 minutes. Let stand until cool.

Drain the pineapple, reserving the juice. Add enough water to the juice to measure 2 cups. Combine with the pudding mix and gelatin in a saucepan. Bring to a boil over medium heat, stirring constantly. Pour into a bowl. Chill, covered, until thickened. Fold in the whipped topping.

Pour the pudding mixture evenly over the prepared crust. Sprinkle the pineapple over the top. Chill, covered, for 2 hours or until firm.

YIELD: 9 SERVINGS

LARRY W. BLACK
STATION 33

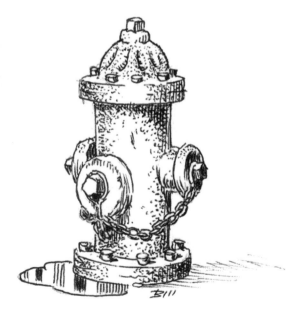

Rita's Delight

1 (20-OUNCE) PACKAGE CHOCOLATE WAFER SANDWICH COOKIES
½ GALLON CHOCOLATE ICE CREAM, SOFTENED
2 (16-OUNCE) CANS HERSHEY'S CHOCOLATE SYRUP
1 SMALL JAR HONEY-ROASTED OR SALTED PEANUTS

Crush the cookies. Sprinkle over the bottom of a 9×13-inch dish. Spread the ice cream evenly over the crushed cookies. Pour the syrup over the ice cream. Sprinkle the peanuts over the top. Freeze, covered, for 4 hours or longer.

YIELD: 15 SERVINGS

ROBERT G. PARRY
EMS

Applesauce Fruit Cake

3 CUPS SIFTED FLOUR
1/2 TEASPOON SALT
1 1/2 TEASPOONS BAKING SODA
1 CUP CHOPPED DATES
1 CUP CHOPPED RAISINS
1/2 TO 1 CUP CANDIED FRUIT
1 CUP CHOPPED NUTS
1 CUP (2 STICKS) BUTTER,
  SOFTENED

1 1/2 CUPS SUGAR
2 TEASPOONS CINNAMON
1 TEASPOON CLOVES
1 TEASPOON ALLSPICE
2 EGGS
2 (16-OUNCE) CANS APPLESAUCE

Sift the flour, salt and baking soda together. Combine 1/2 cup of the sifted dry ingredients with the dates, raisins, candied fruit and nuts in a bowl and toss to coat.

Cream the butter, sugar, cinnamon, cloves and allspice in a mixing bowl until light and fluffy. Beat the eggs in a mixing bowl until foamy. Add the beaten eggs and sifted dry ingredients alternately to the creamed mixture, mixing well after each addition. Stir in the applesauce and fruit mixture. Pour into a greased and floured bundt pan.

Place a pan of water on the lowest oven rack. Bake the cake at 325 degrees for 2 hours or until cake tests done.

YIELD: 16 SERVINGS

KENNETH M. BOLES
STATION 103

DESSERTS

Chocolate Sheet Cake

2 CUPS FLOUR
2 CUPS SUGAR
1 TEASPOON CINNAMON
½ CUP (1 STICK) MARGARINE
3½ TABLESPOONS BAKING
    COCOA
½ CUP SHORTENING

1 CUP WATER
½ CUP BUTTERMILK
2 EGGS
1 TEASPOON BAKING SODA
1 TEASPOON VANILLA EXTRACT
CHOCOLATE PECAN ICING

Combine the flour, sugar and cinnamon in a bowl and mix well. Combine the margarine, baking cocoa, shortening and water in a saucepan. Bring to a boil, stirring frequently. Pour over the dry ingredients and mix well. Add the buttermilk, eggs, baking soda and vanilla and mix well; the batter will be thin. Pour into a greased and floured 11×16-inch baking pan.

Bake at 325 degrees for 20 minutes. Pour the Chocolate Pecan Icing over the hot cake. Serve warm or cooled with vanilla ice cream.

YIELD: 40 SERVINGS
CHARLIE AND LINDA WILSON
FIRE ALARM

Chocolate Pecan Icing

1 (1-POUND) PACKAGE
    CONFECTIONERS' SUGAR
½ CUP (1 STICK) MARGARINE
3½ TABLESPOONS BAKING
    COCOA

⅓ CUP MILK
1 CUP PECANS

Place the confectioners' sugar in a bowl. Combine the margarine, baking cocoa and milk in a saucepan. Bring to a boil, stirring frequently. Pour over the confectioners' sugar and mix well. Stir in the pecans.

Mississippi Mud Cake

1 CUP (2 STICKS) MARGARINE
2 CUPS SUGAR
1/4 CUP BAKING COCOA
4 EGGS
1 1/2 CUPS FLOUR

1 TEASPOON VANILLA EXTRACT
1 1/2 CUPS CHOPPED PECANS
1 (13-OUNCE) JAR
   MARSHMALLOW CREAM
CHOCOLATE ICING

Heat the margarine in a saucepan over low heat until melted. Cream the sugar, baking cocoa and melted margarine in a mixing bowl. Add the eggs 1 at a time, mixing well after each addition. Add the flour and mix well. Stir in the vanilla and pecans. Pour into a greased and floured 9×13-inch baking pan.

Bake at 350 degrees for 30 minutes. Set the jar of marshmallow cream in hot water and let stand until warm. Spread over the hot cake. Spread the Chocolate Icing over the marshmallow cream.

YIELD: 15 SERVINGS

GABINO "GABE" CORTEZ
ARSON

Chocolate Icing

1/3 CUP BAKING COCOA
1/2 CUP EVAPORATED MILK
1/2 CUP (1 STICK) MARGARINE,
   MELTED

1 (1-POUND) PACKAGE
   CONFECTIONERS' SUGAR
2 TEASPOONS VANILLA EXTRACT

Combine the baking cocoa, evaporated milk, margarine and confectioners' sugar in a bowl and mix until smooth. Stir in the vanilla.

Extra-Board Pound Cakes

2⅓ CUPS FLOUR

1 TEASPOON BAKING POWDER

½ TEASPOON SALT

⅔ CUP BUTTER OR MARGARINE, SOFTENED

1½ CUPS SUGAR

3 EGGS

¾ CUP MILK

Combine the flour, baking powder and salt in a bowl and mix well. Cream the butter and sugar in a mixing bowl until light and fluffy. Add the eggs 1 at a time, mixing well after each addition. Add the dry ingredients and milk alternately, mixing well after each addition.

Pour equal portions of the batter into 3 buttered and floured loaf pans. Bake at 350 degrees for 1 hour or until a wooden pick inserted in the centers comes out clean.

YIELD: 30 SERVINGS

LARRY REISS
STATION 49

Sunny Apple Spice Cake

5 CUPS CHOPPED UNPEELED APPLES	1 TABLESPOON BAKING POWDER
3 TABLESPOONS CINNAMON	½ TEASPOON SEA SALT
1 TABLESPOON ALLSPICE	1 CUP GOLDEN OR OTHER RAISINS
1 TEASPOON CLOVES (OPTIONAL)	¾ CUP CORN OIL
3 CUPS WHOLE WHEAT PASTRY FLOUR	1 CUP BARLEY MALT
	1½ TO 2 CUPS WATER
	SUNFLOWER KERNELS OR NUTS

Combine the apples, cinnamon, allspice and cloves in a bowl and mix well. Let stand until the apples have absorbed the spices. Add the pastry flour, baking powder, sea salt and raisins to the apple mixture and mix well. Add the corn oil, malt and water and mix well.

Spoon the batter into an oiled and floured 12-inch springform pan. Sprinkle the sunflower kernels over the top. Bake at 350 degrees for 45 to 60 minutes.

YIELD: 10 TO 12 SERVINGS   FAMILY OF KIMBERLY SMITH

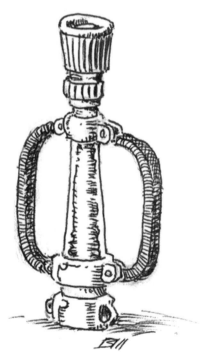

Sticky Pecan Cake

6 EGG WHITES

3 CUPS PACKED BROWN SUGAR

2 CUPS FLOUR

2 TEASPOONS BAKING POWDER

PINCH OF SALT

1 TEASPOON VANILLA EXTRACT

3 CUPS PECANS

Combine the egg whites and brown sugar in a bowl and mix well. Add the flour, baking powder, salt and vanilla and mix well. Stir in the pecans.

Spoon the batter into a greased and floured cake pan. Bake at 250 degrees for 2 hours or until the cake tests done.

YIELD: 8 TO 12 SERVINGS

DOUG LEWIS
STATION 81

Old-Fashioned Tea Cakes

3 EGGS

3 CUPS SUGAR

¾ CUP BUTTERMILK

1 TEASPOON BAKING SODA

1 CUP SHORTENING

2 TEASPOONS VANILLA EXTRACT

FLOUR

Combine the eggs, sugar, buttermilk, baking soda, shortening and vanilla in a mixing bowl and mix well. Add flour gradually, mixing well after each addition until of the consistency of cookie dough.

Roll ¼ inch thick on a lightly floured surface. Cut into 1-inch squares. Bake at 325 degrees until golden brown.

YIELD: VARIABLE

DOUG LEWIS
STATION 81

Light Pudding Pie

2 (6-OUNCE) PACKAGES INSTANT
    PUDDING MIX, ANY FLAVOR

2 CUPS 2% OR SKIM MILK

8 OUNCES WHIPPED TOPPING

1 BAKED PIE SHELL OR PIE
    SHELL FLAVOR OF CHOICE

Combine the pudding mix and milk in a bowl. Stir until the pudding is almost set. Add the whipped topping and mix well. Spoon into the pie shell. Chill, covered, for 3 hours or longer.

NOTE: A good combination is a chocolate pie crust, white chocolate pudding and chocolate chips sprinkled over the top.

YIELD: 6 SERVINGS

HECTOR QUIAN
STATION 49

Banana Caramel Pie

1 (8-OUNCE) CAN SWEETENED CONDENSED MILK
2 BANANAS
1 BAKED (9-INCH) PIE SHELL OR GRAHAM CRACKER PIE SHELL
WHIPPED TOPPING
NUTS

Pour the condensed milk into a pie plate. Cover with foil and place in hot water. Bake at 425 degrees for 1 hour or until thick and caramel colored.

Slice the bananas and arrange over the bottom of the pie shell. Pour the caramel over the bananas. Spread the whipped topping over the caramel. Sprinkle the nuts over the top. Chill, covered, until ready to serve.

You may substitute chocolate pudding for the bananas to make a chocolate caramel pie.

YIELD: 6 SERVINGS

BRIAN BATTENFIELD
STATION 17

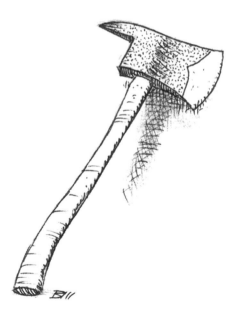

Fire Station 17

Station 17, just east of downtown across from the famous original Ninfa's restaurant, houses an engine, ambulance, rehab truck, an HPD SWAT vehicle, a rescue boat, and "Big Blow" (a motor used to ventilate at large fires). Opened in 1982, this building replaced the original station opened in the early 1900s. Not to forget their history, the crews keep an old wood burning stove sitting by their ice machine on the apparatus floor. Though they have big plans to mount it on bricks, they have yet to do so. Their favorite meals are enchiladas, fried chicken, and spaghetti.

Chocolate Cream Pie

²/₃ CUP SUGAR

¹/₄ CUP CORNSTARCH

¹/₂ TEASPOON SALT

2¹/₂ CUPS MILK

2 OUNCES UNSWEETENED
    CHOCOLATE

3 EGG YOLKS, BEATEN

1 TEASPOON VANILLA EXTRACT

1 BAKED (9-INCH) PIE SHELL

3 EGG WHITES

6 TABLESPOONS SUGAR

Combine ²/₃ cup sugar, cornstarch and salt in a 2-quart saucepan and mix well. Add the milk gradually, stirring until smooth. Cook over low heat, stirring constantly. Add the chocolate, stirring until smooth. Stir a small amount of the hot chocolate mixture into the beaten egg yolks; stir the egg yolks into the hot chocolate mixture. Bring to a boil over medium-low heat, stirring constantly. Boil for 1 minute. Remove from the heat. Stir in the vanilla. Cover the surface with waxed paper or plastic wrap. Let stand for 1 hour or until slightly cooled; do not allow to stand for more than 1 hour. Spoon into the pie shell.

Beat the egg whites in a mixing bowl until soft peaks form. Add 6 tablespoons sugar gradually, beating until stiff peaks form. Spread over the filling, sealing to the edge. Bake at 350 degrees for 15 to 20 minutes or until light brown. Cool at room temperature away from drafts.

YIELD: 8 SERVINGS

LARRY W. BLACK
STATION 33

DESSERTS

Key Lime Pie

2 TEASPOONS UNFLAVORED
   GELATIN
½ CUP KEY LIME JUICE
1 EGG
1 EGG YOLK
1 (14-OUNCE) CAN
   FAT-FREE SWEETENED
   CONDENSED MILK
¼ CUP COLD EVAPORATED
   SKIM MILK

1 TEASPOON GRATED LIME ZEST
   (OPTIONAL)
1 (9-INCH) REDUCED-FAT
   GRAHAM CRACKER PIE SHELL
10 EXTRA-THIN KEY LIME SLICES
10 MINIATURE MERINGUES
   (OPTIONAL) (AT RIGHT)

Sprinkle the gelatin over the lime juice in a small bowl. Let stand for 5 minutes or until softened. Stir the gelatin into the lime juice until dissolved.

Beat the egg and egg yolk in a large heat-resistant mixing bowl for 5 minutes or until thick and pale yellow. Beat in the gelatin mixture and condensed milk at low speed until mixed. Place the bowl over simmering water; do not allow the water to touch the bottom of the bowl. Cook for 10 minutes or until heated through and thickened, stirring constantly; do not boil. Remove from the heat. Chill, covered, until the mixture begins to set. Beat at high speed until light and creamy.

Beat the evaporated skim milk in a mixing bowl until doubled in volume. Fold the beaten milk and lime zest into the gelatin mixture. Pour into the pie shell. Chill, covered, until set. Arrange the lime slices around the pie. Place a Miniature Meringue on each slice.

YIELD: 10 SERVINGS

MICHAEL PLUMMER
CENTRAL COMMAND

Miniature Meringues

1 EGG WHITE
PINCH OF SALT
4 TABLESPOONS SUGAR
¼ TEASPOON VANILLA
   EXTRACT

Beat the egg white and salt in a mixing bowl until stiff peaks form. Beat in 3 tablespoons of the sugar gradually until the egg white is very stiff. Fold in the remaining 1 tablespoon sugar and vanilla. Spoon into a sealable plastic bag. Seal and cut ¼ inch diagonally from a bottom corner. Squeeze the bag over a baking sheet covered with waxed or parchment paper, forming ¾-inch circles.

Bake at 275 degrees for 40 minutes or until dry to the touch and light brown. Remove to a wire rack to cool completely. Store in an airtight container or freeze tightly covered.

Fire Department Definitions

Heavy Box—A fire response of four engines, two ladder trucks, two district chiefs, one safety officer, one EMS supervisor, and the closest ambulance.

High Rise Box—A response of five engines, three ladder trucks, three district chiefs, one safety officer, one EMS supervisor, and the closest ambulance.

Million Dollar Pies

8 OUNCES WHIPPED TOPPING
1 (14-OUNCE) CAN SWEETENED CONDENSED MILK
1 (4-OUNCE) CAN SHREDDED COCONUT
1 (16-OUNCE) CAN CRUSHED PINEAPPLE, DRAINED
1 (3-OUNCE) PACKAGE CHOPPED PECANS
JUICE OF 1 LEMON
2 (9-INCH) GRAHAM CRACKER PIE SHELLS

Combine the whipped topping and condensed milk in a bowl and mix well. Add the coconut, pineapple, pecans and lemon juice and mix well. Pour into the pie shells.

Chill, covered, for 8 to 12 hours.

YIELD: 12 SERVINGS

JANICE AND ANTHONY RUSSO
VAL JAHNKE TRAINING ACADEMY

Chocolate Walnut Cookies

2 CUPS FLOUR	2 EGGS
1 TEASPOON BAKING POWDER	2 OUNCES UNSWEETENED
1/2 TEASPOON SALT	CHOCOLATE, MELTED
1/2 CUP SHORTENING	1/3 CUP MILK
1 2/3 CUPS SUGAR	1/2 CUP CHOPPED WALNUTS
2 TEASPOONS VANILLA EXTRACT	CONFECTIONERS' SUGAR

Sift the flour, baking powder and salt together. Cream the shortening, sugar and vanilla in a mixing bowl until light and fluffy. Add the eggs and mix well. Add the chocolate and mix well. Add the sifted dry ingredients alternately with the milk, mixing well after each addition. Stir in the walnuts. Chill, covered, for 3 hours.

Shape into 1-inch balls. Roll in confectioners' sugar to coat. Place 2 to 3 inches apart on a greased cookie sheet.

Bake at 350 degrees for 8 to 10 minutes. Cool slightly on the cookie sheet. Remove to a wire rack to cool completely.

YIELD: 2 DOZEN COOKIES

LARRY W. BLACK
STATION 33A

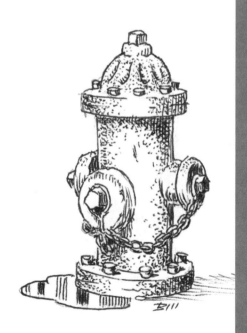

Cocoa Kahlúa Pecan Biscotti

½ CUP (1 STICK) BUTTER OR
  MARGARINE, SOFTENED
1 CUP SUGAR
2 EGGS
1½ TABLESPOONS KAHLÚA
2¼ CUPS FLOUR

1½ TEASPOONS BAKING POWDER
¼ TEASPOON SALT
1½ TABLESPOONS BAKING
  COCOA
½ CUP PECANS

Cream the butter and sugar at medium speed in a mixing bowl until light and fluffy. Add the eggs and mix well. Stir in the Kahlúa.

Combine the flour, baking powder, salt and baking cocoa and mix well. Add to the butter mixture and mix well. Stir in the pecans.

Divide the dough into 2 equal portions. Shape each portion into a 9×12-inch log and place on a greased baking sheet. Bake at 350 degrees for 30 minutes or until firm. Cool on the baking sheets for 5 minutes. Remove to a wire rack to cool completely.

Cut each log diagonally into ½-inch-thick slices. Arrange the slices on baking sheets. Bake at 350 degrees for 5 to 7 minutes. Turn the slices over and bake for an additional 5 to 7 minutes. Remove to a wire rack to cool completely.

YIELD: 2½ DOZEN BISCOTTI

DENISE AND RICHARD MANN
STATION 10

DESSERTS

Magic Cookie Bars

¾ CUP SUGAR

¾ CUP DARK CORN SYRUP

¾ CUP CHUNKY PEANUT BUTTER

4½ CUPS CORNFLAKES, CRISP RICE CEREAL OR GROUND OAT CEREAL

¾ CUP PEANUTS OR BROKEN MIXED NUTS (OPTIONAL)

Combine the sugar and corn syrup in a saucepan and mix well. Bring to a boil over medium heat, stirring constantly. Boil for 1 minute. Add the peanut butter and mix well. Stir in the cornflakes and peanuts and mix well. Press over the bottom of a greased 9×13-inch pan. Let stand until cool. Cut into bars.

YIELD: 4½ DOZEN BARS

LARRY BLACK
STATION 33

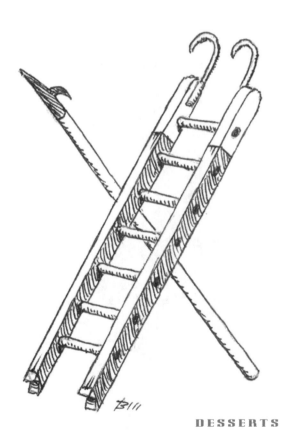

Outrageous Praline Bars

¾ CUP (1½ STICKS) BUTTER OR
    MARGARINE, SOFTENED
½ CUP SUGAR
½ TEASPOON VANILLA EXTRACT
1½ CUPS FLOUR
16 OUNCES CREAM CHEESE,
    SOFTENED

½ CUP SUGAR
½ TEASPOON VANILLA EXTRACT
2 EGGS
½ CUP ALMOND BRICKLE CHIPS
3 TABLESPOONS CARAMEL ICE
    CREAM TOPPING

Cream the butter, ½ cup sugar and ½ teaspoon vanilla
at medium speed in a mixing bowl until light and fluffy. Beat
in the flour gradually at low speed. Press over the bottom of a
9×13-inch baking pan. Bake at 350 degrees for 20 to 30 minutes
or until light brown.

Beat the cream cheese, ½ cup sugar and ½ teaspoon vanilla
at medium speed in a mixing bowl until well blended. Add the
eggs and mix well. Stir in the almond brickle chips. Pour evenly
over the crust.

Dot the top of the cream cheese mixture with the caramel
topping. Draw a knife through the caramel and cream cheese
mixture to create a marble effect. Bake at 350 degrees for
30 minutes. Cool on a wire rack. Chill, covered, in the
refrigerator. Cut into bars.

YIELD: 2 DOZEN BARS

HOBERT HOGGARD
STATION 16

DESSERTS

Brownies

½ CUP (1 STICK) MARGARINE, MELTED

1 CUP SUGAR

2 EGGS

½ TEASPOON VANILLA EXTRACT

¾ CUP FLOUR

½ TEASPOON BAKING POWDER

½ TEASPOON SALT

⅓ CUP BAKING COCOA

Combine the margarine, sugar, eggs and vanilla in a bowl and mix well. Combine the flour, baking powder, salt and cocoa in a bowl and mix well. Add to the sugar mixture and mix well. Pour into an 8×8-inch baking pan.

Bake at 350 degrees for 30 minutes or until the brownies pull from the sides of the pan. Serve with vanilla ice cream. You may double the ingredients and bake in a 9×13-inch baking pan.

YIELD: 16 BROWNIES

ROGER WESTHOFF
STATION 49

Mouthwatering Brownies

1½ CUPS FLOUR

1 TEASPOON BAKING POWDER

1 TEASPOON SALT

4 OUNCES UNSWEETENED
  CHOCOLATE

10 TABLESPOONS BUTTER

2 CUPS SUGAR

4 EGGS

1 TEASPOON VANILLA EXTRACT

PECAN HALVES

Combine the flour, baking powder and salt in a bowl and mix well.

Combine the chocolate and butter in a saucepan. Cook until melted, stirring frequently. Remove from the heat. Add the sugar and mix well. Add the eggs 1 at a time, mixing well after each addition. Stir in the vanilla. Add the flour mixture and mix well. Pour into a greased 9×13-inch baking pan.

Arrange the pecan halves over the top of the batter. Bake at 350 degrees for 30 minutes or until the brownies pull from the sides of the pan.

YIELD: 15 BROWNIES

ROBERT MARLEY
STATION 23

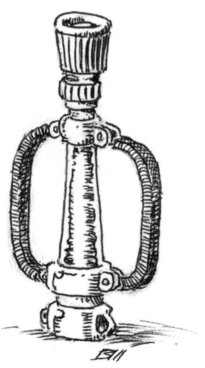

DESSERTS

Chocolate Peanut Butter Balls

4 CUPS CRISP RICE CEREAL
2 (12-OUNCE) JARS PEANUT
    BUTTER
1 (1-POUND) PACKAGE
    CONFECTIONERS' SUGAR
½ CUP (1 STICK) MARGARINE,
    SOFTENED

6 OUNCES SEMISWEET
    CHOCOLATE
8 OUNCES MILK CHOCOLATE
½ (4-OUNCE) CAKE PARAFFIN

Combine the cereal, peanut butter, confectioners' sugar and margarine in a bowl and mix well. Shape into small balls.

Heat the semisweet chocolate, milk chocolate and paraffin in a double boiler. Cook until melted, stirring frequently.

Place a wooden pick in each ball. Dip in the warm chocolate mixture to coat. Place on waxed paper. Let stand until set.

Do not substitute butter for the margarine in this recipe.

YIELD: 4 DOZEN

ANDY COE
STATION 16

Contributors

*Thanks to the following for contributing recipes, stories,
ideas and other material to the book.*

Paul Aguirre
Lonnie Alexander
Bill Baldy
Lary Batiste
Brian Battenfield
Boe Beaty
G. Bennett
Rick Berlanga
Harvey Birdwell
Larry Black
Keith Bobbitt
Jeff Boles
Kenneth Boles
Joseph T. Bond
Kelly Bost-Chandler
Steve Bradford
Pat Brown
Ben and Janette Brymer
Robert Buchman
Karen Cambias
Mike Cannon
Aurora Carrasco
Toni Cartwright
David Childers
John Christopher
Steven Cichon
Andy Coe
Al Cogbill
Greg Collins
Jeff Cook
Daniel Corona
Eddie Corral
Gabe Cortez

Randall Currie
Debbie Davids
Russell Dunnem
James Eli
Tommy Erickson
Jay Evans
George Fress
Les Fulgham
Michael Gann
Mike Girardi
Clyde Gordon
Scott Grant
Ronald Grimstead
Frank Grizzaffi
Julissa Guerrero
Nick Guillen
Ed Guissinger
Jim "Big Dog" Harling
Lil Harris
Lester Harvey
Donnie Havemann
Eddie and Lisa Havlice
Butch Hayes
Lydia Henn
Hobert Hoggard
Robert Hoggard
Linda Honeycutt
Billy Hunt
Mike Hutchens
Larry Hunter
Edward Johnson
Nancy Kamman
Gene Kendall Sr.

Contributors

Al Kiel
Steve Kramer
James Ledbetter
Steve Levell
Doug Lewis
Dina Lira
Terry Litzinger
Howard Livesay
Richard and Denise Mann
Robert Marley
Daniel Matt
The family of Lewis Mayo
David McBroom
Larry McClure
Donnie and Becky McComb
Brian McLeroy
McLeroy family
Juan Mendoza
Bruce Mitchell
Kevin Morrin
Cheryl Morris
Steve Newsome
Robert Parry
David Persse, M.D.
Gary Pick
Michael Plummer
Ennio Ponte
Hector Quian
Larry Reiss
Raymond Richardson
Raul (Gooley) Rivera
Ann Marie Rodriguez
Anthony and Janice Russo
Glenn Rust
Daniel Salazar
Lisa Simmons

Marshall Simmons
Trey Sleet
The family of Kimberly Smith
Diana Faye Steward
Larry Smith
Kevin Therault
Linda Evers Trippodo
Chris Tyra
Lester and Emily Tyra
Larry Vackar
Val Jahnke Training
Academy staff
Terry Vick
Jerry Walker
Llewell Walters
Rick Watterson
Roger Westhoff
Charlie and Linda Wilson
Gretchen Wolf
Merrill Wood
Rickey Wood
Al Young
Mary Delphine Zarsky

STATION 20 SMOKE DIVERS
STATION 7C
STATION 17
STATION 21
STATION 27A
STATION 40D
STATION 51C
STATION 71
STATION 76A
STATION 81

Index

Index

Index

Index